WAVE BARRACKS 232

B.J.Murray

Order this book online at www.trafford.com
or email orders@trafford.com

Most Trafford titles are also available at major online book retailers.

Printed in Victoria, BC, Canada.

ISBN: 978-1-4269-2213-8 (sc)

ISBN: 978-1-4269-2214-5 (dj)

Library of Congress Control Number: 2009912361

Our mission is to efficiently provide the world's finest, most comprehensive book publishing service, enabling every author to experience success. To find out how to publish your book, your way, and have it available worldwide, visit us online at www.trafford.com

Trafford rev. 03/29/2010

www.trafford.com

North America & international
toll-free: 1 888 232 4444 (USA & Canada)
phone: 250 383 6864 • fax: 812 355 4082

Contents

...

Chapter 13
Vance

Chapter One

Boot Camp

ainbridge Maryland Naval Training Station boot
mp was totally not what Cheri had been expecting. The walls
ere barren, the floors were washed out plain wooden planks
erything was grayish in color. The room was full of small iron
uble bunk beds with exposed coiled springs each held a wafer
in mattress' that was rolled up at the foot of them. There was
multitude of black ominous looking metal lockers placed about
e room and they were all six feet tall.

The room was quite shaded on this late fall afternoon because
was very cloudy outside, and it was chilly in the building; after
it was the end of October and the heat had not been turned on
t. There were several small windows in the large room but they
ere placed up high and close to the ceiling, you would be able
see what the weather was by looking at the sky, but you would
t be able to see what was happening at the ground level. Cheri
ought this placed looked and felt like what prison probably was
e: lonely and cold. The Wave in charge of indoctrination of
w recruits told them to put their suitcase on a bed, just pick one
y one, because the one you pick is yours for the next thirteen
eeks, and then she told them to assemble in the Day Room.

The Day Room was a large room filled with leather couch and chairs which held females of all shapes and sizes and they we all white, except for Cheri whom they chose to ignore like she w invisible. The girls were chattering nervously amongst themselv asking each other where they were from making small talk ar giggling nervously. Cheri was tired and hungry and irritable aft riding the train for a day and a half it had been a long tireson trip, so she didn't care if they talked to her or not since most them from what she could see were homely looking anyway.

When they had finally arrived at the train station in Marylar were they had to disembark from the old train they were glad get off of it, it had been culture shock to go from the sleek tra they had originally rode on. When Cheri and the other two gir she had left the city with heading to Bainbridge Maryland th had ridden on a sleek shiny silver train called the Zephyr, th had their own individual compartments and a porter had broug their meals to their compartment and had come back later in t evening to turn the seats down into a bed. But the next mornir they were told that they would have to transfer to another train get to their final destination. The train they transferred to was a old rusty train with a pot belly stove in the center of the car whe they were seated. The seats were very hard made of some kind basket weave material, what happened to the luxury?

Cheri and the other two girls that had been sworn in wi her at the Navy Department the day before then had to stan around outside the train station and wait for another hour for t base bus to come and pick them up and take them to the Nav Training Station.

Cherilyn Adams had left home feeling proud like she w somebody, now she only felt dread of what was to come. Had sl made the right decision to join the military? Here she was in th unfamiliar place with all these strange young women and noboc knew anybody. They had all come from different parts of the countr and no two people were from the exact same place; they had con from the same state but different cities and towns in the state. Che decided then and there that she would do what she had to do and l the best she could be to survive this messed up situation.

After an hour of milling around in that room it was announced
er the Public Address System that effective immediately all
'ave Recruits were on a diet. What did that mean? This was
believable! Cheri only weighed 109 lbs and she felt she would
obably get thinner than she already was. Then they were told
"Muster on the Grinder" in 10 minutes for lunch. To "Muster
the Grinder" meant going outside and lining up by height to
lk over to the Mess Hall for lunch. Once they went outside the
rracks they had to line up as best they could and that was when
ey noticed there was about fifteen to twenty other companies
girls lined up as far as the eyes could see to their left, dressed
gray uniforms and carrying flags, the shortest girls in front and
e line graduated back to the tallest girls bringing up the rear. The
w girls found out soon enough that you ate by seniority, not by
10 got to the door first and since they were the last Company to
me in for training for another two weeks, they were considered
e "Baby Company" and to wait and do everything last.

In Boot Camp the "Baby Company" had to wait until all the
her companies had entered the Mess Hall and had eaten their
eal and come out before they could go in to eat they were always
st. Some days they had to stand outside for over an hour, waiting
go in to eat. After standing outside in the chilly fading sun they
ally got to go inside the Mess Hall; this is where they would
ve all their meals during their thirteen weeks of training.

The Mess Hall was a huge one story building with a long line
steam tables situated in the center of the room, you took a metal
ıy and some silverware at the door and walked down the line of
eam tables just holding your tray out in front of you for what you
ınted, and you didn't ask for anything and you did not speak to
e men dishing out the food. The room was equipped with rows
d rows of picnic style tables with the benches attached so you
d to step over into them to sit down. They were forced to eat
at awful bland meal which was totally devoid of any butter or
asoning, because the waves were on a diet. The men dishing out
e food had been given instruction of what to give the women, so
ey got a very limited amount of food and no deserts.

The mess hall was flooded with roaches, there were so many
them they were literally falling from the ceiling as they sat the
and tried to eat. Cheri felt the food was not fit to eat and sl
didn't want it. If they had these many roaches visibly how mai
were cooked in the food? Cheri just drank some cold milk and a
a plain dinner roll, she had lost her appetite from the appearan
of this place; she couldn't eat in there, she wasn't use to eating
this kind of environment.

After the horrendous experience in the mess hall they we
herded back to the Day Room, were they were each given a stenc
and a white and black marking pen. They were told to stencil the
names into the clothes they had brought and to keep the penci
safe, because they would have to use them on their uniforn
when they got them. They had been told to bring five white slip
five pairs of white panties, five white brassieres, two garter bel
two pairs of pajamas, a robe, and a pair of house slippers, also
weeks change of clothes, two pairs of shoes and their cosmetic
stenciling their clothes kept them busy for a while.

The wave in charge gave them a set of rough cotton shee
and a thin cotton bedspread and told them to make up their bec
Cheri had opted for the top bunk she didn't want anybody sleepir
over her, those mattress were so thin that if the person had a be
wetting problem you would surely catch it. After struggling
make up their beds they were told that the beds had to be ta
enough for a quarter to bounce off of it, and the corners were
be squared and that was to be expected from them for the ne
thirteen weeks. So the girls started working together as a tea
since it would take two people to pull those sheets and bedsprea
tight enough for a quarter to bounce off it.

The girls had also noticed that some of the companies carrie
flags in front of their platoons when they marched. So they aske
the wave in charge about it and were told that only the "Smarte
Companies" on the base got to carry the flags everywhere the
went because they had proven themselves superior to everyboc
else by earning the flags.

There were three flags they could earn; the "I", and the "C
and the "A".

The flags represented, "I" for intelligence, your company got is flag for passing the weekly tests with high scores, the "C" ıg was for cleanliness, if your company passed inspections ery week and the "A" flag was for all around excellence in erything, so in order to really shine your company had to udy hard and get high marks on all the test they would be king every week, pass all inspections and just be the best of ıe best which meant tight team work, so the strong would ıve to help the weak in-order for their company to qualify r flags, this taught them self discipline and teamwork which mes in handy in life.

It didn't matter what the weather was you dressed in what ou were told to wear over the PA system first thing in the orning, when they shouted **Reveille** to wake them up. Since aves do not carry umbrellas; and you could only wear what ıe uniform of the day was there was a lot of chaos those first w days. If it was raining, snowing or hot as hell you wore what ou were told, not what you wanted to or what you felt like you ıould wear. If the uniform of the day was gray dresses and veaters that's what you wore even if it was snowing outside, ıis was to teach them self discipline. If it was pouring down ining and they didn't announce "raincoats" you didn't wear ne you just got wet, they pulled these stunts on them until the rls got the hang of doing what they were told. Since Cheri's roup was the "Baby Company" they felt self conscious because ıey had to wear their civilian clothes for a whole week and a alf. The babies stuck out like a sore thumb on the base in the ifferent styles and colors of their clothing, they had not been niformed yet, and being fitted for your uniforms would take week or more. It was rough trying to march in heels and oking so rag tag.

Cheri couldn't wait to get her uniforms and put on the gr seersucker dress with the black necktie and garrison cap just she would fit in. She thought the gray stripe seersucker dress looked terrific, they buttoned up the front and had short sleev and they were snug in the waist with an A-line skirt, compare to the civilian clothes they were wearing. Some girls had on lo cut blouses, all kinds of colorful skirts, high heel shoes; some the girls including Cheri, had been thinking and had broug flat shoes along with their other clothing. The clothing they ha brought was stylish for the time, but it was stuff that would hav been more appropriate in civilian life. So here on a military ba were everybody else was in uniform they looked totally out place and they stuck out like a bunch of country bumpkins. Eve though everybody here had gone through the same process th still couldn't help feeling awkward like they didn't really belon they felt like the ugly duckling before it was transformed into beautiful swan.

That first week was filled with all kinds of orientations, goin for medical and dental examinations. The hardest part of militar life that took the most getting use to was the lights being turne off at 2200 hrs(10:00pm) by a recording of taps, and then bein awaken with somebody shouting Reveille over the PA syste every morning at 6:00am. The baby company was being fitte for their uniforms by this loudmouthed older wave that was ov the clothing department. She was short and stubby and her ha looked like a brillo pad. She had a big mole on her jaw with hai in it and she wore wire rim glasses. She had a very gruff an rough demeanor and was down right homely to look at. Sh would ask them what size they wore and then she would han them sets of clothing two sizes to big, telling them they woul grow into them.

Some of the girls realized the best way to deal with her was t to argue with her, just do a lot of swapping among themselves ıen they got back to the barracks. Some of the girls would eak down and cry because their clothes were way too big, and eir shoes were either too big or too small. It was like she was tfitting them for the circus to work as clowns, and was getting personal kick out of making them look and feel bad. This senior ive would referred to them as "Queenie" when they didn't move act fast enough for her, but at the end of the thirteen weeks of ining they realized she had been an angel in disguise. She was ice, sweet, caring person who was extra hard on them to make em shape up and be the best that they could be. After they rted shaping up she let them know she was a real person with elings and a bright smile.

They were told they would have to hem their gray seersucker esses themselves, and they were to stencil their names in all of eir new uniforms. That's when the crying really started and did t let up. Some of those girls could not sew, and they had never wn in their lives. Cheri made a lot of money hemming their ersucker dresses, even though the stitches were more than an ch long. That first week more than eight girls left to go back me, they couldn't take all that rough living and bad treatment, ey said they were homesick so the Navy sent them back home; t Cheri was not a quitter she wasn't going anywhere she was re for the long haul. The uniform department was responsible r hemming their dress blue serge uniforms, so in order to make eir skirts fit properly, they wouldn't button the skirt at the waist, ey would then pull the waist down as low as they could get it on eir hips while the seamstress was pinning up the hem.

They did this so that when she finished hemming their skirts ey would fall just below their knees and would not be hanging lf way down their legs like an old lady. The crafty girls learned ick how to circumvent the system, especially since it was stacked ainst them so they did what they had to do to survive because ey refused to be at the mercy of the Navy.

Chief Kaiser was assigned to oversee the training of Cher company which was Company 35, she decided on her own assign this big burly, red headed, blue eyed, cankle legged, co fed girl from Iowa to be her mouth piece, unbeknown to the re of the company. This girl was suppose to oversee them and mak sure they did what they were suppose to do and go where the were suppose to go on time. The reason for her choosing th particular girl was because of her size, she was the biggest one the group; and to take some of the pressure of training the gir off of the Chief. Basically the girl was the sheep herder and the were the sheep, being herded from place to place all day long.

Cheri who was always conscious of her appearance, and alwa took the extra time she needed to make sure everything on h was in its proper place before going outside to muster and fa her public. Cheri had to make sure her hair was pinned up ju so and her makeup was put on properly, so she was always the la one to come out of the Barracks for muster in the morning, sh wasn't late just always last. On the morning of the third day boot camp here comes "Corn Fed", stomping down the woode plank floor passing all the rows of empty made up bunk beds unt she got to Cheri's bunk

Which was located in the back of the room; then she stoppe and flashed her big blue eyes at Cheri and shouted as loud as sh could "**get outside**" **NOW**! Cheri turned from looking into h small compact mirror which she had propped up against the be railing and the pillow; so she could see herself while groomin and said in a low steady voice "**get out of my face, you don't te me what to do",** "Corn Fed" dropped her eyes turned on her hee and retreated from the area.

After they had their breakfast that day the Chief sent for
ieri to come to her office. When Cheri arrived; the Chief told
r to take a seat which was across the desk from her, of which
ieri did. Then the Chief leaned half over her desk and stared
enacingly at Cheri and said I was told that you did not obey a
rect order today. Cheri looked that woman square in her eyes
d said what order? The Chief said one of my aides asked you
go outside to muster and you refused why? Cheri said that
rl" does not tell me what to do, we got here at the same time,
the same day, and she has the same "rank" that I do, which is
ecruit". The Chief was taken aback and quite surprised with
ieri's answer, (most new recruits were so afraid of authority of
y kind that they would take orders from a mouse).

The Chief sat back in her chair and drumming her fingers
the desk said you know you are right! You did get here on the
me day and you are the same rank, but I made her an Officer
the company yesterday. I can do that, I have the authority to
that, I am in charge of this company; but since you feel that
ongly about it I'll make you a deal.

I need help, a lot of help, making sure you eighty-seven girls
were they are suppose to go and do what they are suppose to
, so if you want to help me accomplish that task I'll be glad to
ake you an Officer too. The Chief told Cheri it would be her job
see that the flags were raised and lowered in the morning and
ening and put away and she would also be responsible for going
the base Post Office and getting the mail and distributing it to
e girls and to just basically help keep them in line. I just need you
generally help keep this Company running smoothly. Cheri said
ight and effective day three of boot camp Cheri was an Officer
her Company and when they got their new blue uniforms, Corn
ed and Cheri had emblems sewn on their suit coat sleeves to
stinguish them as officers over the others in the Company. Corn
ed and Cheri ran Company Thirty-Five together for the next
elve weeks and had mutual respect for each other.

Laundry day was on Mondays you stood in line with yo
dirty linen in your arms and turned it in to the same loud mouth
Senior Wave (she was a Non Commissioned Officer but since th
had not studied ranks yet they just thought she was a senior wav
that had been in charge of issuing them their uniforms. She wou
take their sheets and shake them out for all to see on the floor ar
if they had any stains or dirt on them you would get demeri
Demerits meant that you had to go clean the classrooms all d
on Saturday which was one their off days. Cheri got chocola
on her sheets once and only once from eating a candy bar in b
after taps (lights out), she had smuggled it out of the "G-Dun
(the base recreation hall and store where they could buy hoste
cupcakes and assorted candy bars and sodas).

Cheri got five demerits for that chocolate stain and aft
that backbreaking weekend she spent mopping and waxing ar
buffing the floors, she never did get another one. The rule whi
seemed crazy to them at the time was your linen had to be as cle
when you turn it in as it was when you got it. Cheri felt it was
crazy rule; but something that they would just have to learn to li
with after all this was the Navy not their homes. Whoever hear
anybody sleeping on linens for a solid week and them being ju
as clean when you turn them in as they were when you got the
that sounded plain nuts. But they learned that if you keep yo
body clean and your hair clean by taking a shower every nig
and in the morning if you need it, and by washing the makeup o
their face before they retired for the night their linen will still
clean. It was later that they learned that if they didn't have rul
some of those girls would have been absolutely ridicules.

Most people have a tendency to be slouchy and trifling, an
if they are not trained as a child to be clean and tidy, when th
become adults they have the same old habits they have lived wi
all their life which are hard to break because they just don't care, it
all they are use to. So a course in hygiene is essential for everybo
that way nobody can feel picked on, and everybody benefits. T
shower area was one big windowless room with a multitude
spigots coming out of the walls; there were no shower curtains
stalls to hide in, all modesty is out the window.

Cheri was constantly being looked at especially since she was
e only black girl, it was a good thing she had a serious attitude
ıd a thick skin otherwise they would have gotten under it.
obody gave any thought as to why the Chief always seemed to
peared when it was time for them to take their showers, before
ey went to bed and after their

Swimming lessons, no one tried to figure it out as to why she
uld manage the time to come in and chit chat with them while
ey were taking a shower, could it have been she had a preference
r young girls? Was she getting her kicks looking at all eighty-
ven of those young nubile girls while acting as their Superior
fficer and nobody was the wiser?

Some of the girls were from the Deep South and had never
aternized with blacks, had never really paid them any attention,
Cheri was like a mystery, a science project to them. After a few
ıys all those girls warmed up and they all became fast friends.
ıe Chief told them they would become like sisters. Cheri had said
ıo way", but after living with eighty six other females twenty-four
ven for thirteen weeks you do become bonded, because she did.

One girl in particular was fascinated with Cheri. She was
short girl with naturally curly short blonde hair and sky blue
'es and the deepest southern accent you ever heard. She became
heri's best friend and running buddy all through boot camp,
er name was Pricket and she was from Gadsden, Alabama. They
ecame inseparable, they were like Siamese twins, they would
udy together and shine their shoes together, do their laundry
gether and go over to the G-Dunk for recreation together, were
ey would buy packs of cupcakes and candy bars and hide them
their Ditty Bags to eat later; because there was no refrigerator
go back to if they didn't like what they were having for dinner
ıd got hungry later. The girls would also hide contraband in
ıeir laundry bags, since the Chief rarely checked the laundry
ıgs this was the perfect hiding place.

They knew the Chief made impromptu inspections of the quarters while they were out and they were not allowed to ha that stuff in their locker, they could buy it and eat it immediate but were not allowed to store it. Pricket invited Cheri to g home with her after they graduated from Boot Camp. They we planning to travel to Alabama and then go on to Pa. to Cher house, but Cheri's mother who had been born in the south, to her not to go to Alabama so that plan was quashed. So th had a good friendship for the twelve weeks wrote a few lette back and forth telling each other about their new duty statio and moved on with their lives after all they had just been frien not lovers. During their free time when the smoking light w lit which was once every evening for fifteen minutes, Cheri ar another girl named Dorothy sat and wrote the Company thir five song together, it was turned in and accepted and printed ar the girls sang it daily while marching.

Marching and singing was a requirement in the military, if you feet were bad, too bad, if your shoes were too small, so what! G over it, March, your left, your left, sing and March on. Cheri ha deep feelings of patriotism it just felt good to be in the military a suited up, marching, singing and studying, and dealing with th everyday bullshit of learning how to sit and rise from a chair like lady. How to only cross your legs at the ankles not over your kne like a man, you are not a man. They were instructed that waves a ladies and they were to act like a lady at all times while workin towards their graduation and after they got to their permaner duty stations. After six weeks you get the option of going to g the dances that where held on Friday nights or you could opt t go to the show on Saturday afternoons.

Waves weren't allowed to speak to men in boot camp, it wa called "**skylarking**", and if you were caught looking at or talking t the men you would get demerits. For getting demerits you kne you would have to clean a building on the weekend instead c doing whatever you wanted like studying, relaxing or doing you laundry at the base laundry house or visiting with other waves i another company on base.

They had to study every night because they had classes Monday ru Friday to learn about the military and the different branches ' the military and the different ranks, and how to spot them. ıey had to learn a lot of stuff that they really had no interest in ıt they had joined so they had to do what they were told and ıat was expected of them. They also had to learn how to do their vn personal laundry there are no maids in the military, some of ose girls Cheri included had never had to do laundry. Cheri's other always did the family laundry she didn't know anything out it but she learned. They all learned how to starch a collar so rd that when you wet it and pressed it, it was like cardboard, you uld thump it with your fingers and it made a hard noise. The ost important thing they learned was how to march in cadence; ey finally did learn their right from their left, and how to make ose sharp turns on a dime it was a beautiful sight to behold, but wasn't easy because a lot of the girls Cheri included didn't know eir left foot or hand from their right. Since they were basically ing on restriction to them every guy that worked in the mess ıll was a John Derek look-a-like, even if realistically he looked ce the Son of Kong. Because they were not allowed to look at talk to a man except when they went to the dances that was all ey wanted to do.

They had all picked out a boyfriend from the guys they saw the mess hall and the ones that served them their food or the ıes they saw at the matinee on Saturday afternoons. The only oblem was the guys had no idea they were some young girl's ntasy. Cheri and her close buddies went to the dances a few mes wearing their gray seersucker dresses and beige cotton ocking and old lady black lace up oxford shoes, trying to attract e attention of some young man. After attending a few of the ınces and making small talk with the guys who were there; heri found the dances boring, she didn't like the music and she dn't know these guys and the guys didn't know her and that was ıe, because the few guys she had met so far were not her type. was all a game they played to help pass the time and the dances ere always highly chaperoned. You got to interact with the male ecies for a few hours without getting demerits.

Some of the girls started writing to the different guys th
had met at the dances, Cheri couldn't imagine writing to someo
who lives less than fifty yards away, to her that was stupid. Che
and her real close buddies preferred attending the matinee
the base theatre on Saturday afternoons. Once there they wou
make fifty trips up and down the aisles in their old lady outfi
but they felt they were alluring and could be sexy in anything
was all about attitude.....When you can wear a gray and whi
pinstripe seersucker cotton A-line dress paired with a navy bl
cardigan sweater and pale tan cotton stockings (they only came
one shade) and black lace up oxfords with the one and a half inc
heel and still feel sexy as hell, and think some guy wants you, yo
have a dynamite opinion of yourself.

Whenever a Senior Company would get their orders (marchin
papers) to their new permanent duty station, it made you sad
see them go but it also made you glad, because you knew that yo
were moving up a notch closer to becoming the Senior Compan
You were becoming more and more polished every day learnin
what you needed to learn, things were getting easier and you we
heading towards your own graduation and being a real workin
part of this man's Navy. The girls in Cheri's Company we
constantly telling her that she was pretty and talented and becaus
she could sing and dance so well; that she should have been i
show business. Cheri knew that it was common knowledge
this time in the sixties that American's only felt blue eyed blond
were the epitome of beauty.....so if these country white girls we
that impressed with her especially the ones from the deep sout
she must really be raising hell....so evolved her attitude.

At boot camp you had to prepare for inspection every week d whoever got "Sharp Wave" at every inspection through out e twelve weeks would receive the "**American Spirit Award**" graduation. Cheri wanted that award. She dreamed about tting it at night and she was determined to get it come hell high water. She always had her collars starched to perfection her snow white shirts; her navy blue uniform was impeccable, mpletely lint free. She was always making sure the knot in r tie was tied perfectly squared. Cheri made sure there was no ake-up on the inside of her hat, by not applying make-up to r forehead, and making sure to always wear her hair up off her llar and have her white gloves bleached as white as can be.

Cheri would give her shoes such a high shine you could put makeup with them, she would be up in the lavatory late at ght after the lights had been turned off in the dorm, sitting the cold concrete floor by the only light left on (the one in e lavatory was left on in case someone had to make a call of ture during the night) with a small tin of hot water (the tin as the lid of the shinola shoe wax can)and equipped with a bag cotton balls and their cans of Shinola shoe polish Cheri and icket would be shinning their shoes or studying out of their ue Jackets Manual for the next days classes or getting ready r the constant inspections. They inspected everything, your bed w it was made up; your locker to see if your clothes were hung properly and the shirts and jackets were buttoned and facing e same way, even when they were hanging on a hangar in the cker so many rules.

There were three grades you could get at the weekly inspectio: the best was Sharp Wave, the next one was Excellent, and th third was Good, Cheri did not want anything but Sharp Wa she needed all Sharpe Waves to get that award, she wanted th award worst than Ray Charles wanted to see, she wanted to g home with the American Spirit Award that would be great. Yo had to line up by Companies and stand at attention for the L to come through the ranks and check you out. Cheri knew ho to handle inspections she knew the drill just stand there ar look straight ahead and don't lock your knees so you don't c off your circulation and faint. So after the Lt had circled her f the "fourth" time Cheri knew in her gut that this "bitch" was n going to give her "Sharp Wave", she was looking for any excuse not give her what she knew she deserved and what Cheri kne she had coming.

The Lt. finally removed Cheri's hat and said get a haircut ar rated her "excellent". Cheri wanted to cuss that bitch out but sh knew she couldn't, so she just took it like the sailor she was, suc it up and kept on keeping on. At the graduation ceremony th gave the American Spirit award to some nondescript quite type girl that could have easily faded into the woodwork from Orego Cheri was disappointed she should have gotten that award an the other girls in her group even said so. There was nobody i that Company or on that base at that period of time for th matter that had more heart than she did, she should have gotte it just for the pressure she had been under the first few weeks, th constant stares, the isolation, had it not been for her attitude sh would have buckled after the first two days how could that not b the American Spirit..

Once you graduated from boot camp you would be going in tally different directions, scattered to the four corners of these nited States it was all temporary all bullshit they give shit to 10ever they want to, not to who deserved it so she shrugged off and stayed focused. To Cheri, military life was a transient estyle, you meet you greet and you get orders to go some place se at a moments notice it was like living as a gypsy. Cheri found is aspect of it attractive, here today there tomorrow. For now heri had to get through the business of finishing up boot camp. udying into the night trying to remember the different insignia's d stripes for rank. Learning all the working parts of a ship and plane, the different types of ships, how to tell a Submarine from Dingy, they had class five days a week, and it was imperative that ey all passed so their Company could get the flag for intelligence, they helped each other study at night and on the weekends d before they were midway through their training, Co 35 was arching all over the base singing and carrying all four flags right in front of their Company until the day they graduated and ft the Naval Training Base at Bainbridge, Maryland.

The one area that was the biggest problem Cheri had to ercome was to quality swimming. Everyday they had to go the indoor pool and practice swimming for two hours. The ol area was a huge building that housed the pool, the showers d lockers. And since the walls were mostly made of glass they ere always steamed up, the room just felt moist and had a strong lorine smell. The dept of the pool ranged from 3' to 12' of water. heri did not know how to swim, she had spent many summers ing to the beach daily and wading in the water or floating in an ner tube; so she was not afraid of the water, she just never had ken the time to learn to swim.

Qualifying swimming was part of the training and if you did ot quality swimming you would not be graduating with your ompany. They would keep putting you in different companies ntil you learned to swim or until they got tired of fooling with ou and gave you a discharge.

How can you be a sailor and sail aboard a ship out on th oceans and seas and not know how to swim? Cheri had it a mapped out in her head, her Company was to graduate the wee of Christmas; therefore she would be able to be home for th holidays before reporting to her new duty station. Cheri and th other waves would go over to the pool for two hours every da they would take the required shower then suit up in the one pie tank suit made of some kind of flimsy cotton jersey material. A flaws were extremely noticeable; this suit had no shape and n built in's.

Instead of practicing swimming as they were suppose to b doing, they would sit on the side of the pool dangling their leg and feet in the water and kibitzing about whatever was on the minds. They used this time as some kind of leisure social perio until it got down to the wire. It was three weeks before graduatio and the number of non-qualified swimmers was down to s and they still had to come to the pool area daily Cheri include because they had not qualified swimming. Once you qualifie swimming you were not required to go to the pool, you could us the time for whatever you chose to do with it. This particular da they went thru their usual ritual of getting in the pool to wet the suits, and then proceeded to get out and sit on the side of the poo with their legs crossed talking amongst themselves, that's whe the Captain and two of her Lt's came walking by. They stoppe and asked the girls when they were going to qualify swimming?

Then they told them that if they didn't qualify they woul not be graduating with their class, they would have to stay her on base until they did, meaning no graduation at Christmas fo them. Well that put a different spin on the situation, Cheri said sh was going to qualify tomorrow; which meant she was just stallin for more time and they knew it. Meanwhile a few diehards wer taking turns standing up on the Pink Elephant (the diving boar was painted pink) with rosary beads in their hands praying fo the strength to jump off into the water, while the instructor stoo below them with a six foot pole in her hand trying to coaxin them to jump, she would use the pole to pull them out when the started to drown.

The Pink Elephant was 8' high from the floor and hung out er the pool, so when you stand up there and looked down it ade the pool look like a postage stamp, it made you feel like if u jumped you might miss the pool all together and bust your ad open on the tile edges surrounding it. The purpose of all is height was suppose to simulate the height of a ship, this was actice for when if ever they had to jump overboard from the le of a ship. Cheri and Pricket thought this was funny as hell tching those girls standing way up there crying and trembling ey felt this was pure entertainment should be better than the eatre. The instructor had been watching them from the corner her eye making fun of the others, so she called Cheri over and ked her when she was going to qualify?

Always the one to detect when someone is trying to call her it, Cheri said loudly "**right now**", so after the trembling girl scended down the stairs of the pink elephant, Cheri boldly imbed up to the top of the Pink Elephant. This was the first ne in her life of ever going up on a diving board, but she did it cause she had more than her share of heart. As Cheri stepped it to the edge of the pink elephant and stood there they started chant, jump, jump, jump, so Cheri shouted count, and as they arted to count they only got to count to two before she stepped f the pink elephant and went straight down into the 12' ft of aiting cold water.

"**Splash**", the water split apart from the weight of Cheri's body tting it feet first, as she sank lower and lower into the water, heri was holding her breathe and fighting the urge to panic as e water filled her nostrils and ears, she could hear her own heart ating like a drum, it seemed like an awfully long time until r feet finally felt the pool floor beneath them, opening her eyes e realized she could see, so she just relaxed and let her body go np as she pushed up with her toes with all her might letting her dy's natural buoyancy take her back to the pool surface.

When she broke through the surface and could see the ceilin of the pool area, she leaned back like she had been taught to c and started to do the back stroke, this was the stroke they ha been taught to use by the instructor while lying on the floor by th pool, but she had never used it before in the water. She stroke so hard that instead of going the length of the pool and turnin around and coming back she went the length and the whole sid before coming back to the side of the pool by the Pink Elephan and climbing out. Everybody who had been watching startin cheering, Cheri felt so good; she was out of breathe but she wa done with that damn pool and she never again wanted to see th Pink Elephant in life. Most importantly she wouldn't have put on that flimsy, jersey ill-fitting swimming suit and tremb in that cold filthy water until her body became acclimated to th temperature.

The wind was whipping their faces, it was bitter cold out an snowing as they walked back to the barracks from the pool it wa December in Maryland. Cheri was freezing cold but inside sh was warm and happy she had finally made it! And she was gla it was over if she had known it would be that easy she woul have done it weeks ago. After spending twelve weeks on that sh she was feeling elated even though her hair was sopping wet an heavy with pool water. The swimming cap the Navy issued ha given her zero protection from the water it was good for absolute nothing, and to top it off her hair smelled like chlorine, but Che didn't mind that either; she would just have to shampoo her ha herself tonight she thought.

As they walked and talked and laughed about the extra lengt of the pool she had swam out of fear, she felt so good she wante to jump with joy. Cheri told them that her sole purpose was t hurry up and get out of that filthy water, and try not to drink an of it, she had seen snot floating in that water on more than on occasion and there was no telling how many people had peed i it out of fear.

Chief Kaiser, the barracks chief was also elated when they came to the barracks and told her Cheri had qualified swimming, she d had a sinking feeling that Cheri wouldn't make her graduation cause of her fear of swimming. Smiling she told Cheri her hair oked like it could use a good shampoo, so would you like me to ake a call and see if I can get you an emergency appointment day with the base beautician to get your hair styled? Cheri id that would be great because they were having their first ofessional pictures taken in two days and she didn't want to ok like some village had lost its idiot on her pictures. As picture king day came and went Cheri's hair was still looking nice while me of the other girls looked like they were on retainer to haunt operty for Halloween. Cheri still had to pin her hair up in e back, she mostly wore it in a French twist because she could it her garrison cap over the roll in back and it still looked neat. 'aves can not have their hair on their collars and she refused to t it cut on the base, because the haircuts she had seen on some the other girls the last few weeks were not becoming to them at ; and she had no desire to walk around looking like a displaced erson, so she wore it pinned up or curled so tight it was off her llar, but at least it was clean and not smelling like chlorine.

Chapter Two

Wave Barracks 232

"SAN FRANCISCO" THE CONDUCTOR CALLED out loudl that's when Cheri stood up and started to gather her belongin to disembark from the train she had been riding for three day she was so excited she could hardly contain herself. She said h farewells to the cute young soldier she had shared the coach sea with, (after all they had slept in each others arms for two nights, is inevitable that when two people share coach seats and fall aslee they are going to wake up in each others faces and they did). The had talked for two days about any and everything just to break tl monotony of the long train ride. She had found it interesting th he was a reader like herself; he was reading a book on "Hawaii He was traveling on to Stockton and she was getting off, this wa finally her stop, San Francisco, California. Cheri's dreams we finally coming true, California, where you could wear summ clothes all year around and they say you can pick oranges off th trees and eat them. Hollywood was not that far away either an she might get to see some of the movie stars she had seen i the movies since this was the land of fantasy. Cheri knew Sa Francisco was not Los Angeles, but she knew she was a lot clos that if she had still been in Pittsburgh, Pennsylvania.

When Cheri stepped off the train and looked around she was rely disappointed, it was not at all like she had imagined, and was so foggy you couldn't see more than a foot in front of you. was damp and a chilly light drizzling rain was falling, having ly her uniform raincoat for warmth, she begin to tremble as is chill went to the bone. It was only 6:00pm in California and eady it was dark, damp, chilly and foggy this was definitely lture shock, somebody had done a lot of lying in the brochures out sunny California.

After collecting her suitcase from the baggage handler, Cheri lked out to the cab stand to hail a cab, requesting the driver take her to Treasure Island Naval Base. The cab drivers have system for military bases they like to fill up their cabs before ey take off, so she waited in the cab, while the driver rounded several more fares that were also going to the base or going that general area, after he loaded up his fares they took off for eir destinations. Sitting in the backseat of the cab peering out the grimy window at the passing traffic and going over one ng bridge after another San Francisco didn't look like much of ything; Cheri thought to herself that she should have picked other city, maybe, San Diego, or even another state like Corpus hristi, Texas.

She had been asked to make three choices of where she wanted go two weeks before graduation and California had been one them, as they say watch what you wish for. Cheri had wanted go where it was sunny and warm so she could bask in the heat, t were it was cold and damp like this. But she made a promise herself, that she would go to the base and do whatever it took be the best that she could be, she would not let an adverse tuation get her down.

She was a fighter, she would make it. She would work real rd, and get to Officers Candidate School and go overseas to urope or the Orient anywhere to get away from this dismal ty.

Cheri did not like cold damp weather, maybe it was becau
she was so thin that she was basically cold all the time, even in t
summer sometimes she felt chilly and would wear a sweater, ar
when she bought clothes she always made sure she got dress
with jackets or two piece outfits for layering, and a lot of blaze
that she would layer with pleated skirts. In the summer she wou
buy light weight linen jackets to go over her linen pleated skir
plus she was self conscious about her figure, being so slender,
size four or six did not make you voluptuous.

Cheri had learned how to camouflage her ultra slim figu
by only wearing full skirted dresses or styles that were flatteri
to her body type, she never wore sleeveless tops or low cut to
because she thought her arms were too skinny and her brea
were too small and she didn't like her collar bones to show, whi
women today kill or starve themselves to death to see.

"THROUGH THESE GATES WALK THE WORLDS FINEST"

At least that's what the sign said hanging above the entrance the main gate of the base. Treasure Island Naval Station oked impressive with the sharp marines standing guard in their ess blues at the gate, maybe things would be looking up after all heri told herself. She decided to look on the bright side. Cheri t proud and a little depressed; proud because she knew she cut a e figure in her dress blue uniform and bucket hat, white gloves, ack spit shined pumps and purse, with her raincoat over her m.

After all just like the sign said the worlds finest and she was one them, everybody couldn't pass the test to get into the military, d there had been a lot of them, you had to take a battery of e hard tests to get in, and each one was easier than the last, she essed that was to weed out the undesirables up front.

Cheri was a little depressed over the weather she hated gray ys, they brought her spirits down she was a sunshine girl she dn't curl up and do nothing when it was gray, but she just eferred the sun. Cheri paid the driver her portion of the cab e since she was sharing the cab and retrieved her luggage; wished her luck as he sped off to drop off some sailors and arines at their barracks on the base. Upon exiting the cab in ont of Wave Barracks 232 Cheri was disillusioned at what she w in front of her, was this a joke or what? It looked like a nch of cheap wooden row houses all of them in need of a good at of paint or something to brighten them up. And they were aced in a square with the front porches facing each other like a compound. Cheri later learned that this was called the Wave ompound. The only light leading up to the double front doors as a lone lamp hanging from the wall of the building, there was ree wide wooden steps leading up to the front doors with a ngle railing to hold on to, the railing was damp to the touch.

This place looked pretty damn dismal and there was not soul to be seen anywhere in sight. Cheri walked up the stairs ar opened the door and entered the building, she approached tl Master-at-Arms desk and gave her name and rank and request permission to come aboard of the girl behind the count Permission granted she gave the Master-at-Arms her orders ar proceeded to check in.

She was assigned a temporary room since there had been large influx of new Waves over the New Year and since she w one of the last few to sign in she was placed in the transient dor Cheri was feeling almost depressed with her new surrounding a barren room with four iron bunk beds stacked on top of ea other separated by a desk and a chair, one dresser and four met lockers to share with heaven only knows who. The bed was n made so she would have to go and request bed linens and make u her bed for later. While standing in the middle of the floor tryi to make sense of this place and get some order in her life for tl moment Cheri decided to hang up her clothes. She noticed the were no hangers in the metal lockers and hearing voices comi from the next adjoining cubicle she decided to go over and a them if they had any spare hangers.

As she pushed open the door of the locker this big bon brown skin girl with a better than average looking face and a he full of curly hair turned and fixed her large slightly hooded ey on Cheri, it was apparent she was holding court over the assort motley crew of girls who were sitting on the beds and the flo staring up at her with adoration, as she stood in the middle of tl floor, Cheri said hi and asked her if she had any extra hangers ar the girl said "**you knock before you come in here**". Cheri w slight in built but no lightweight in the bully department, she w a bully herself when she chose to be and she was use to standi her ground.

Also she didn't appreciate the fact that this big dufus bitch as trying to call her out in front of this bunch of country ass tches she was entertaining. Cheri said loud and clear "**Fuck u**" and turned around and left the area leaving the locker doors pen. That was the start of a friendship that would last a lifetime. heri and the barracks bully Mia became the best of friends. See s all about attitude……..

Cheri returned to the hole of a room she had been assigned stay in and she was furious, she was so mad she wanted to hurt mebody. She didn't sign up for all these disappointments, but e had to put her feelings aside for the moment because she was ying to figure out how she was suppose to hang up her clothes th no damn hangers. This didn't make any kind of sense, how the hell are you suppose to function when you can't even hang you damn clothes.

"**BANG**" the doors of the metal lockers flew open (they ways kept the two set of doors open for privacy) Cheri turned d looked up from unpacking her suitcase to see Dora standing ere "hey girl" what's happening? Before Cheri could answer ora said grinning at her I've been waiting for you to get here. heri said as far as I can see nothing is happening yet.

They had met during the last weeks of boot camp at the eekly "Sing Along" held in the GeDunk. In fact they had been competition against each other. When the Company Officers und out they had people who could sing they always wanted em to sing and entertain them and the rest of the company like ey were at a concert. That was how they had met and discussed here their new duty stations were going to be. Dora had told heri she was going straight to the base after graduation and ng out until after the New Year. Other than that Cheri knew othing about this funny looking girl.

Cheri told Dora she needed some hanger's bad, if for nothing se but to hang up her uniforms. Cheri had to report for work rst thing in the morning and she didn't plan to go on a new job oking like a wrinkled up hobo.

Dora said wait a minute girl calm down, just cool your je
she could tell by Cheri's tone she was upset and getting more
by the minute, so she turned and left the cubicle and return
a few minutes later with a bunch of hangers in her hand whi
she handed to Cheri. Cheri thanked Dora for the hangers ar
started unloading her trunk. Cheri said to Dora while hanging u
her clothes what's going on around here? Dora's eyes lit up li
light bulbs as she said everything girl, I have been scooping o
the base waiting for you.

Dora said everybody congregates at the EM Club (Enlist
Men's Club) at night do you want to go tonight? Cheri said
don't know, I guess, but I have to report for work in the mornir
and I need to take a shower and get my clothes pressed, they a
wrinkled as hell from being packed up for so long (Cheri ha
shipped her trunk on ahead to the base while she was on tw
weeks leave at home over the Christmas holidays). Dora showe
Cheri where the laundry room was and told her how to opera
the washer and dryer and introduced her to the ironing board ar
irons so she could iron her clothes. After pressing her unifor
and a white shirt for the next day, Cheri made up her bed for th
night; then she went to take a much needed shower after ridir
for three days on the train and sleeping in a chair.

After her hot shower Cheri felt better and started to get reac
to go to the club with Dora. Cheri was pondering over what
wear to the club when Dora reappeared, after picking out a
outfit to wear a green wool two piece outfit with a white oxfor
buttoned down shirt. The top was a weskit type vest the skirt wa
pleated, which she wore with color coordinated matching gree
shoes (Cheri was and always had been a sharp dresser).

Cheri prided herself on her wardrobe; she had lived in Ne
York prior to joining the Navy so she had a lot of 5th Avenu
clothes, Cheri use to spend her whole paycheck shopping. Th
girls and guys in her hometown use to call her New York becaus
of her wardrobe. Cheri had more civilian clothes than any c
those girls on base had ever seen before in their lives.

Dora was literally drooling out of the side of her mouth hile fingering the different fabric and styles as she supposedly as helping Cheri hang up her clothes, all the while thinking to rself how she would become tight with this girl. Dora felt if ey became best buddies then she could ask to borrow some of ese gorgeous outfits they were about the same size, but Dora uldn't do anything with Cheri's shoes, Cheri wore a size six oe and Dora wore a nine.

After they finished hanging up most of her clothes and ran t of hangers, the rest Cheri put in the dresser drawers for the ne being. Then Cheri turned and told Dora she had to work her hair, if she was going to the Club with her that night so e needed to be pulled together. Cheri then asked Dora to leave r room and give her some privacy; so she could put on her derwear and finish getting herself together. Dora left Cheri's om with the understanding they would meet in the lobby later t she said to herself as she left; I don't know if I can be friends th this snotty bitch, she was almost border line rude to me, lling me I have to go while she gets dressed, after I helped her s out with hangars and shit who do she think she is? Cheri had en a bootleg beautician back in her hometown and her hair as always well done, she didn't feel comfortable unless she felt r attire and her hair was just so then she would feel pride in rself.

Cheri hated people who were self-conscious she sensed they ly felt that way because they felt inferior, so if you have no flaws hy feel inferior? Cheri had a problem with people who went it with seams busted and hems hanging down, something being ld up with a safety pin. She felt that even if you couldn't see it e knew it was there and that made her nervous, and she didn't ce being nervous she always wanted to feel in control of herself at's why she didn't drink or take drugs.

Wrinkles in clothes were definitely out of the question, take t
time to press them don't just throw on anything and go somepla
If she didn't have enough notice to prepare herself properly, s
wouldn't even attend a function she rather stay home. This mig
sound shallow to some people but to Cheri it was a way of li
She was raised to take pride in herself and her work. Cheri did
think anybody was better than she was, and most of them not h
as good. She felt that from the way she looked and dressed a
took care of herself that if a guy didn't want her he was either
freak or a phony.

CHAPTER THREE

The Enlisted Men's Club

ORA AND CHERI MET UP at the Master-at-Arms desk and alked the three blocks over to the Club they arrived in good irits. The EM Club was a building on the base that catered to listed men only. It had a takeout restaurant in the front managed a man name Bart. He was a sailor by day and manager/short der cook at the Club at night. You could order pizza, beer, ft drinks, tacos, hamburgers and steak burgers, everything was oked to order by Bart and his helpers, Bart was dating several the waves but his favorite was Fanny.

The Club was a hit and it was always packed to capacity cause it was the only place the enlisted personnel could go and nce and drink. The beer was the biggest seller since it only cost 0 cents a pitcher and the pitchers were large enough so that at ast four or five people could drink from it and get drunk. The nce area; which was a huge room filled with tables and chairs d a raised stage off to the side for the live entertainers that rformed on the base on Saturday nights. During the week it as jukebox only. After the girls ordered their beverages from the staurant area, they walked in and found themselves a table and arted to sit down with their drinks.

Cheri had a coke because she didn't drink. Dora who w
quite the heavy drinker and smoker had all they had to offer, be
and a pack of cigarettes. One of the first things Cheri had notic
upon entering the Club; was that the females were sitting off
one side of this enormous room and the males were on the oth
She thought it was strange a room full of fine men in assort
shapes, sizes, and colors along with a few dozen attractive femal
and nobody was dancing or talking to each other. Dora and Che
barely got a chance to sit down before they were bombarded wi
offers to dance from all these different guys. The word had gott
around the base that there were new waves on board, so the gu
were waiting like vultures for them to show up and they danc
the night away. Both the girls were good dancers and they kne
all the latest dances so they were a sight to behold.

Dora had had to wear her navy blues to the Club because sl
had no civilian clothes. She was extremely skinny with bowle
(picture two sticks that are bent from the ankle to the thighs tha
what they looked like) now imagine those legs flying all over tl
place with high heels on. Her feet reminded you of a witches fee
long and skinny. Cheri was of medium height but she appear
taller because she walked so straight and she was so slender, eve
though she was slender she was shapely. She had medium leng
black hair, sparkling eyes with long lashes and a small bow mout
that could spew forth pure obscenities. She had beautiful leg
small hands and feet, she had what would be called a delica
bone structure. She was attractive in an exotic way and she w
twenty years old.

She had a superiority attitude towards people she did
know and she had a tendency to look down her nose at strange
especially if they were unkempt. She could give a person such
cold sweeping look, looking them up and down and then aw
like she was dismissing them that it would make them cringe an
want to disappear. She didn't smile much if at all, because she fe
she looked better when she didn't smile, and if she did smile it w
only a small smug smile like the Mona Lisa.

The Club was quite crowded that night and every guy that ›rmally got turned down for a dance, got to dance that night .th Dora and Cheri. They did the Slop, and the Twist, the Uncle 'illie, you name it, they could do it all, because they were good ıncers and they knew it they were from the City not the County. ıey laughed and flirted with all the guys that night it became ‹e a contest to them to see who could do the most outrageous xy dances.

The other waves were sitting in groups whispering behinds eir hands and watching they couldn't believe their eyes. These rls were dancing like they were getting paid and they didn't care ho they danced with. The other waves were shocked! They would :ver dance with the undesirables, if they danced at all. They ostly just came to the Club to sit around and try to look cute ıd make fun of other people. Those waves got a kick out of saying › to some poor sap that had gotten up the nerve to approached em and ask one of them to dance. Cheri and Dora danced with ack guys and white guys, whoever asked, they didn't care.

Cheri wasn't afraid to interact with white people; she had ›ne through school with them and had danced with them as a enager, she wasn't from the south. Cheri saw nothing wrong ith her behavior she wasn't looking for a boyfriend or a husband ıe was just having fun.

When Cheri and Dora left the Club that night they were .famous, the other waves on the base didn't think much of them r dancing with all the undesirable guys, but they didn't care. /ho cares what other females think Cheri didn't she knew they ere just jealous, she was the talk of the base, she had just gotten ıere and she had made a name for herself in one night. She ›uld dance her ass off, she was good looking and she had nice othes and to top it off she started running around with the most ›torious bunch of guys on the base.

The first night she was there she met a guy, Albert he was
undesirable. Al was a handsome marine who had locked his ey
on her as soon as he saw her twirling around on the dance flo
He asked who she was. Nobody knew just some new wave.
wanted her, he was determined she was going to be his girl fir
Al was of medium height about 5'10", brown skinned and he h
a good body. He had hooded eyes which made him look sinist
and thin lips which he kept pursed in a tight line so he looked li
he had no lips at all and was angry all the time. Al was kind of se
in a bad boy way and he was a good kisser. He asked Cheri if
could walk her back to the wave barracks that first night after t
Club closed, she said yes, not knowing he just wanted to establi
to the rest of the guys on the base that she was with him.

On the walk back to the barracks he started grilling her wi
all the usual familiar questions. Where you from? Why are yo
here? Why did she join the Navy? She thought he was kind
cute but a little bit crazy. She told him she was not looking f
a steady boyfriend or a husband. She had joined the Navy to s
the world and have some fun while doing it. Al said he wished
the girls were like her that he was so tired of meeting females a
having them looking at him as a potential husband something
was definitely not ready for yet.

Al and Cheri became a casual item for about two months then got orders to go overseas to Viet Nam. She cared and she didn't re that he was leaving; down inside she was glad. She enjoyed s kisses and his silly jokes but she had just been killing time with m, and lately he had started to get aggressive about her being s girl for real, so she was ready for him to go. She felt relieved ice it was getting to be a real hassle slapping his hands off of her the time. Al was sick and tired of only getting kisses from her, ll! He couldn't even feel her up because he didn't have a car, so he got was the opportunity to walk her back to her barracks night after the club closed. Cheri felt it didn't make sense to t too involved with these guys since everything and everybody as so temporary. Cheri enjoyed them as dance partners but that as as far as it went. So after Al left it was onward and upward they say NEXT.....plus you couldn't trust men in the military, ey would have a wife and several kids at home or wherever they me from and they would lie and say they were single.

It was all about them getting what they wanted when they anted it. While the girl gets all strung out over one of them and inks she is madly in love, then WHAM the bottom falls out, e guy get transferred or is up for discharged and leaves, mostly ider the cloak of darkness.

One minute they are there the next minute they are gone, at's why Cheri and Dora just used them for dancing or a ride to town to get something to eat. Cheri planned on making a reer out of the military and deep down inside she was holding it for OCS (Officers Candidate School) so she could marry an fficer and a Gentleman. Cheri had no desire to be saddled with me young uneducated man whose chances of making a good ing in civilian life were limited. Cheri felt that if the man was Officer that meant he would have been to college and would able to make a good living once he got discharged. After Cheri id joined the Navy and had learned the rules of the military id one of them was Officers do not fraternize with enlisted rsonnel. So she knew the only way to get an Officer was to go OCS (Officers Candidate School).

The enlisted sailors and marines would get drunk as skun
from that .40 cent beer then all hell would break loose; the figh
would break out. Every night it was the same inevitable figh
between the black and white guys. They would carouse arou
together all night until the Club closed then someone wou
make an off colored remark and the fight was on. They wou
fight all the way back to their perspective barracks or until t
Shore Patrol came to break it up or throw them in the brig
sleep it off. They all worked together everyday so they knew ea
other until they got drunk at the club then, it was on again.

One a guy was so drunk walking around in the Club that
threw-up on the floor and just kept walking never missing a ste
Cheri was amazed at how uncouthed the guys were she could
imagine any girl wanting to be married to one of them.

CHAPTER FOUR

The Typing Pool

HERI WAS TO REPORT TO a man named Chief Collins who e would be working for as a typist in the Receiving Station. ıe Chief was a nice man with big discolored teeth that took half his face when he opened his mouth. He was a frail, mild annered black man, who was very nervous and extremely anal out everything. He wanted everything done by the book the M (Blue Jackets Manual) this was the Navy Bible. Everything e Chief gave Cheri to do she did it in record time with no errors d returned it back to him within the hour. The man was going azy looking for things for her to do because he was trying to ep her busy, and he couldn't. He was not use to an efficient orker because most of the people in the military sitting around oing desk work were just killing time until they could retire with monthly pension. The Chief's previous workers had been lazy, ow, shiftless, non-caring people who would take forever to do e smallest task and then they would have to redo it several more nes because of all the errors.

Cheri was wearing the Chief out, as soon as he gave h something to do; within ten to fifteen minutes she was givi it back finished. He wasn't use to having to stop doing wh he was doing to try to find something for her to do; plus sh intimidated him. She had a habit of looking him straight in h eyes which made him even more nervous. He was in awe of ho fast she could type, her little slender fingers would just fly ov the keys so he decided to turned her over to the typing pool th definitely could use the help. The typing pool was a huge roo full of waves and sailors with desks and typewriters spread all ov the place, they spent all day except for breaks and lunch typin discharge and shipping out records for military personnel comin from and going overseas. There were roughly about thirty peop typing in the typing pool area, they typed Monday thru Frid from 7:00am until 4:00pm. The atmosphere in the room was ve relaxed you did your job and spent any free time telling jokes an lies to each other and going downstairs to the little in house ca to get snacks. Everybody liked their job but the work was n getting done, the place was more like a daytime social club.

The Warrant Officer over the Receiving Station was Chi Warrant Officer Dolton. He had several Chiefs and First classme working under him to help him run the different departments i the typing pool. He had two direct reports that he relied on total to keep it rolling while he wallowed in his own world of alcoholisr One was a short fat, pop eyed Mexican named Alvarez who w over the Separation Office for Commissioned Officers, Nora w his typist. The other was a first classman named Quionnes.

Every day the Warrant Officer would go to lunch at eleve o'clock and come back several hours later drunk and he woul sit and sleep at his desk until closing. He was a mild mannere small built man who wore sun glasses and spoke with a souther drawl. He would talk on the phone all morning before going t lunch; so if you wanted him to know or do something you had t get to him first thing in the morning because nothing was goin on in the afternoon with him.

It was understood in the office that if all the work was finished Friday by noon they could leave for lunch and not have to me back until Monday which made for a long weekend. This ln't happen often because a wave name Polly held up production eryday and Friday's were no exception. The men that worked ere didn't care if they got off early or not because most of them ent their time hanging around Polly's desk laughing and talking d smoking, Polly's productivity was zero.

Polly was an exceptionally pretty girl who was quite shapely her six feet tall frame and with her red hair I guess she would called a striking redhead. She had long slightly bow legs and e was from Texas. Polly knew how to work those men, she uld take off her suit jacket and throw her shoulders back so r breast would be straining against the buttons on her uniform irt which should have been a couple of sizes bigger. She would at her desk up front across from Quinnoines and cross her ng legs out into the aisle and blow smoke rings from the ever esent cigarette which dangled from her red lips and talk to the en all day long. The records would get to Polly's desk and that s as far as they got they would pile up on her desk, and since ere was work still to be done the rest of the office personnel uldn't leave for the day. The way the operation worked was ch person would have to add several lines of typed data to the cords. Therefore if one person is holding up the line nobody can ve and everybody had to stay until closing. Cheri didn't like is shit one bit. So one day after she couldn't take it anymore she lked up to CWO Dolton's desk and asked to speak to him. Now is is not done! You are suppose to wait until you were asked to eak to Commissioned Officers. Cheri told him that he needed etter system of handling the typing pool. She explained to him at the work wasn't getting out and she was tried of a few people lding the rest of them back.

CWO Dolton leaned back in his leather padded arm chair cked his fingers behind his head and starred up at her for a few inutes; to Cheri it seemed like forever before he said alright; en you handle it. I am putting you in charge of the typing pool, fective today it's in your capable hands so don't screw it up.

Those waves were furious, the sailors didn't like it either, ju
who does she think she is! Thinking she can come in here ar
take over. How can he put her in charge? She walked in he
three weeks ago from nowhere. Where did she come from anyw
thinking that she can just walk in here and be placed over u
We've been working here for years! The CWO could see wh
he wasn't drunk, that this girl was a good worker she likes to g
things done and she takes pride in her work. She didn't ha
eraser and smudge marks, grease and coffee stains from eating
the records she turned in.

Some of the records that were turned in for him to sign ma
him cringe and he would refuse to sign off on them. The CW
would make a fuss about it then hand them back to Quionnes ar
tell him to have them redone. Cheri had a plan she liked getti
off work at 12:00 noon on Friday and not having to come back
the office until 7:00am on Monday it made for a long weeken
Cheri would count the records that had to be typed that day ar
divides them by how many typists there were. Then she wou
place the stacks of records they had to type on their desks. S
instead of adding a line or two to the records as they had bee
doing and pass it on to the next person, they had to type the enti
record from start to finish. One person would be responsib
for the entire record, therefore; whoever didn't finish their sta
of work had to stay until they did, while the rest of them cou
leave and start their weekend. That started the trend of the enti
second floor of the Receiving Station closing down on Fridays
12:00 noon. The typing pool was running smoother than it ev
had. Quionnes who acted as the Office Administrator over th
pool had a serious attitude about the situation; and he was one
the main perpetrators that spent all his time in Polly's face.

He was a skinny rawboned first classman from the Philippines th a pock marked high cheek boned face, he had haunting deep t black eyes and gold trimmed teeth and he despised black ople. He did not appreciate some young black girl coming into e office and changing things around. It would only take ten to teen minutes of anybody paying attention to see that Quionnes d Alvarez were running the second floor of the Receiving ation and they were doing a very poor job of it.

Since Quionnes and Alvarez had no immediate supervision om the CWO who was always intoxicated and relied heavily them, it was a prime case of the foxes guarding the hen house, pecially since they were all just bidding their time until they uld retire with a full pension while eating the hens one by one.

Everyday there would be new order to cut, papers to be filled it they were processing 200 to 400 military records a day, but matter how many records there were to be processed each day, ey were all divided up by Cheri's rule. Each one of the forms at made up a service record had six or seven sheets of carbons them. Sometimes it would take ten to twelve different forms to ake a service record, and they had to be error free. Anyone who is ever typed knows it's hard to correct a carbon copy and still ive it look crisp and clean, so the best way was to type it error ee, and if you did make an error you start all over again.

Quionnes had such a dislike for Cheri that any mistake he und in her typing he would circle it in red pencil. This infuriated heri, because most of the time it was just a case of her leaving off period or a comma which could have been inserted in jig time, it once you have scrawled all over the six or seven page form ith red pencil that meant the whole thing had to be re-typed ecause of a period. So instead of taking a minute to fix it she id to spend another ten or fifteen minutes to re-type the whole rm. Cheri walked up to Quionnes desk and tried to explained him what he was doing to her productivity and asked that he ot write on the form just bring it back if he found a mistake, he dn't answer her; he wouldn't even look at her, he kept his head own and he never said one word.

Sure enough the next time he found an error on her work l scrawled all over the form for a period she had left off, he made big circle around the space then he brought it over and handed to her not saying one word.

Now Cheri knew for sure that he only scrutinized "her" wo he didn't even look at the others just "hers" because he had hidden agenda. Cheri took one look at the record and she we crazy, it was like flashing a red cape in front of a bull; she was mad she snatched the forms from his hand in one swift motic and slung them behind her into the middle of the receivir station floor, then she and Quionnes exchanged some very lou very heated words. The CWO blinked and staggered up from h chair looking dazed and confused from his nap being interrupte He wanted to know what the hell was going on! And since r one else would speak up; Cheri walked up to his desk and to him; he looked at her and said you can't be insubordinate to yo superior officers.

All eyes were on them, the normal noise of the room we dead silent; the room was so quiet you could hear a rat pissing c cotton. People had stopped moving around it was like they we statues. Cheri stood her ground she was pissed off. She couldr for the life of her understand how the CWO could defend th despicable man, when he knew he was the "King of Fools". Che was smart she had what the military was looking for the on problem was she was a female and they preferred males. She w told all the time by her male counterparts that she would make hell of a shipmate if she was a male.

Cheri said loud and clear, then I "**quit**", nobody is going to as me if I have ever been in the military I'm a female! She snatche her ID card from around her neck and threw it on the CWO desk. The CWO looked down at it for a few second then h sat back down and said "**Pick It Up**" you can't quit, you signe a contract for three years and they are not up yet, then he thre back his bushy head and laughed until his face turned deep re He pulled his hanky from his pants pocket and started dapping his eyes still laughing.

Cheri stood there her chest heaving, her eyes sparkling with ger glaring at the both of them. Then he stood up in front of his air and said in a loud voice for all in the second floor Receiving ation to hear "**Give them hell Cheri Give them hell**", and she d. Polly liked Cheri she was impressed by her spirit. She told r that she was the white queen and Cheri was the black queen d that they could and would make those men do whatever they anted them to do. They became really good friends for about year hanging out at the Club together, bullshitting and doing hatever they could to create chaos.

Polly enjoyed hanging out in Cheri's room and telling her about r latest conquests on the base. Talking about what man she was aking a fool out of, also she got a kick out of mesmerizing the her waves that were doing nothing of notice with their personal es at the hen sessions. She could get pretty graphic about her tics since she got a kick out of shocking people. Polly finally t a live one to go; she met an old Chief who was getting ready retire in a few months and went off to Mexico with him one eekend and got married in a Mexican ceremony.

At the next hen session in Cheri's room the girls started talking out it asking Polly if her marriage was legal in the United States? olly decided to do it again in San Francisco at City Hall just to on the safe side. Polly had come into the Navy with a plan to id an older man that would kiss her ass and give her whatever e wanted financially and so far her plan seemed to be working. ie old Chief had a good pension coming and she felt that being s wife she would help him spend it. She put in for her discharge id left and that was the last time they laid eyes on Polly.

Chapter Five

Barracks Chief

The Barracks Chief was responsible for finding jo for the girls who were stationed on Treasure Island who had r specific job skills or orders for specific job titles when they arriv there for duty, but she took her good ole sweet time doing Cheri had a job waiting for her when she arrived so whatev that woman did to the others girls didn't faze her, it was not h problem. The Chief was personable except she didn't have a cl of how to deal with all those young nubile women, especial since most of them were away from home for the first time their young lives and they were exercising their personal freedo to the fullest extent.

The Chief thought if she became their friend they would confide her and tell her their problems and it would all work itself out in e end **wrong!** Those girls made a fool out of that woman. Cheri ve the Barracks Chief absolutely no respect but she didn't do it on rpose. The woman put herself in such a position that she didn't quire any respect. It was apparent by her actions that the Chief d no feelings for the black waves what so ever, all she wanted em to do was not to cause any problems so she basically left them there own devices. The only waves she laughed and joked around th in Barracks 232 was the handful of resident lesbians from awaii. It was suppose to be her responsibility to see to it that any xually confused individual is expelled from the military, but she ose to play crazy and ignore what was going on.

The only thing she was interested in was checking her sources gularly to find out who was pregnant and get them discharged it of the Navy as soon as possible like quick fast and in a hurry. If girl managed to go the entire pregnancy without being detected d went into labor and was taken to Oaknole Naval Hospital and ve birth there on government soil; "Uncle Sam" was the father! nd that child would be entitled to a government check until it ached eighteen years of age. She felt that pregnant girls were a sgrace to the uniform and should be expelled immediately if not oner. It was also the Chiefs responsibility to assign a room to the w arrivals, grant the wave's permission to go into town, or just ndling any general problems the girls might be experiencing iring their tour of duty.

Cheri stayed in the transient barracks so long it w unbelievable normally you would only have to stay a month ir transient room. Cheri stayed there five months without having real room. She had to deal with all those different women comi back and going overseas. Wac's, Bam's, the married waves that we stationed at Treasure Island but lived ashore with their husban that had to come and spend the night or the weekend on ba because they were scheduled to stand duty as the Master-at-Arr in the barracks. Cheri had to share her living space with all tho strange people, some of them would stay a few days, some a we it was a constant flow of strangers for five long months and t Chief didn't seem to care. There was a Beauty Shop on the ba but there was only one beautician who worked there that cou handle black hair (this was long before they invented perms f blacks) and she was terrible at styling hair.

So the black waves would catch the bus and go into town (S Francisco or Oakland) to get their hair styled at the local beau shops. Generally they washed and rolled their own hair but on or twice a month they liked to go to a professional in town for a c and style or just to feel pampered. So one evening during the we Cheri came into the barracks from work, and as she stopped check her mail she noticed a group of black waves gathered in fro of the Master-at-Arms desk laughing and talking while prepari to leave the base. She asked them where they were going and th said they were going into San Francisco to the beauty shop to g their hair styled, needing a good shampoo and deep condition herself Cheri said wait a minute let me change out of my unifor I'll go with you I need to go to the beauty shop too.

One of the girls said you have to ask the Barracks Chief for ·mission to leave the base you just can't leave; so Cheri walked oss the hall over to where the Barracks Chief was standing ving a conversation with some other waves and said hey I ed to get my hair done, so I need to go into town with them. earing her talk to the Chief like she did the group of waves od there with their mouths hanging open in shock and starring wide eyed disbelief. She was supposed to request permission go ashore; instead she told the Barracks Chief what she was nning to do!

They guess it confused the Chief so much that a new wave d that much nerve, to get in her face and tell her what she was nning to do, that she just said yes, go ahead but next time you :

The girls laughed all the way into town on the base bus. They re laughing at her and with her, but they were also thinking at : same time where did this girl come from? Who in the hell she? They all secretly felt she was the **"mole"** planted in the rracks watching and waiting to snitch on them when they were to no good.

The Chief finally left Cheri a message in her mail box th
she had found her a room and for two months she had a room
herself. Normally there are two waves assigned to each room. T
room contained two oak twin beds, one on either side of the roo
two oak dressers and between the beds was a desk and a chair, to
shared by the room occupants and each room had a stuffed ch
for reading. Over each dresser was a lone lamp hanging from t
wall next to the mirror, there was no pictures on the wall, no extr
and no curtains but you could buy your own personal bedspre
in town if you wanted to. There was a carpet on the floor, but
was not wall to wall so there was a two foot wide border of bla
waxed and highly buffed floor which showed every speck of du
so it had to be kept clean and shiny at all times. Across the ent
way of the room was four mental double door six-foot tall locke
one locker was for your military uniforms and the other was f
your civilian clothes. The doors of the lockers next to the ent
way on either side were kept open to act as an entry door and f
privacy. The lockers were closed during the day when they we
to work, the lockers were closed but left unlocked for impromp
inspections by the Barracks Chief; she wanted to be able to che
for cleanliness and contraband at all times, especially when th
were out of their rooms at work during the day.

When the lockers were closed the doorway was wide open
you could walk down the middle of the passageway and see in
everybody's room just by turning your head from left to rig
Also there were no curtains at the windows just shades. You cou
put the windows up when it was very warm which is not oft
in San Francisco, but since there were no screens on the windo
they would prefer you not to open them.

Cheri would open the windows in her room which was on the cond floor to let out the cigarette smoke when she would hold r hen sessions, they were not suppose to smoke in their rooms, ly in the designated areas. She also would open the windows hang assorted bags of juice, milk or soda pop in plastic bags led with ice outside the window with the window pulled down hold the bag in place. She didn't give any thought to the fact at whoever is walking around the grounds outside could look and see the unauthorized bags of contraband hanging from e window.

They would have gathered up the pop and juice from the nding machines located downstairs in the stairwells when it ould go biz-wacko. Most of the times the vending machine was oke and if you just touched your choice of beverage from the achine, it would continue to spit out whatever you desired until at entire slot was empty and that was when they gathered up e free pop and juice. The word would travel fast among them hen this would happen because those girls would tell each other hen the machine was acting up, they took whatever they could t for free, after all they didn't make much money forty-eight ollars every two week but they did it mainly because they were st plan mischievous.

After two months Cheri got a roommate, a girl from Scotland ith a very heavy brogue accent, her name was Marty Purdy. Cheri ut up with the girl for about three months they didn't really hit off because Cheri couldn't understand what Marty was saying alf the time. Soon Marty started going to the Club every night inking that cheap beer and god only knows what else the men ve her to drink and she started coming back to the barracks oppy drunk. So drunk that she had to be physically hand carried to the barracks and placed in a chair in the lounge.

One night Marty staggered into the room and woke Ch up by throwing-up by the side of her bed right into the carp Now there was only four feet of space separating the two be and this was the undoing of Cheri, when she couldn't take another minute she jumped out of her bed and turned on the lig over her dresser and saw the nasty mess Marty had made on t floor, that's when she started cussing. She told that sick high intoxicated girl that she had to get up and "**Clean That Shit u Right Now**".

Cheri refused to deal with this kind of behavior, she was n going to lay there and smell vomit all night or even stay in a roo with drunken vomit on the carpeted floor. That's when Marty her drunken state tried to comply with Cheri's orders by staggerin up and going down the hall to get a dry bucket and a dry mop, ar when she returned to the room she started to mop the carpet wi the dry mop; while in the process she was strewing her vomit vegetables all over the floor. Cheri was furious; she opened th windows and continued to cuss like the sailor she was, telling th girl that when she came home from work the next evening, sh wanted her drunken ass out of her room.

Cheri gathered her blanket and pillow and relocated to th topside lounge to sleep on one of the cold leather couches for th night. The Chief heard about it from one of the girls that had bee on duty the night before, so she didn't ask Cheri any question she just quietly relocated Marty. At 4:30pm that next evenir when Cheri returned from work, her room in the barracks ha been vacuumed, mopped, waxed and buffed and Marty was lor gone. Cheri rearranged the room just to get rid of the memo of Marty and had her room to herself for the next three or fo months.

Cheri's next roommate was a girl name Alice a tall, thin, pale
·l with dish water blonde hair and gray eyes. She had a slight
.mp in her back from poor posture, which Cheri attributed to
.v self esteem. Alice was real timid and shy, she was sort of on the
·mely side but she had a nice personality. Alice had a boyfriend
10 was also stationed on the base some guy she had met aboard
ip on one of her many assignments so she went out a lot at
ght and on the weekends. Alice was from Mississippi. Her
) on the base was as a Photographers-mate for the Navy so she
s always going off on assignments taking pictures. Alice was a
al good photographer she took clear precise pictures. Alice and
heri shared a room for two months and they got along great
cause Alice did what Cheri told her to; therefore they had no
oblems. Alice liked to take impromptu pictures of Cheri, she
ould catch her coming into the cubicle from the shower in her
be and slippers with a towel wrapped around her head, or she
ould catch her reading with her legs slung across the arm of the
air, or eating with her mouth hanging open in the process of
king a bite of food or while she was sleeping they had lots of
n together.

They enjoyed each others company plus Alice was neat and
ean, she didn't leave her belonging lying around and she kept her
le of the room neat as a pin. Besides Alice didn't drink which
as a big plus factor with Cheri. When Alice got orders that
e was being shipped out on another photography assignment
erseas they were both sad. Cheri missed Alice when she left,
e had been a good roommate mainly because she was gone off
assignments most of the time and she was hardly in the room.
fter those two roommates Cheri had the room to herself until
e met Gina Running Eagle. This girl was a real piece of work
ankfully she was only there for a New York minute.

One evening Cheri comes into her room from work ar
lying on the spare bed was this strange looking female perso
who turned her head and starred up at her. Cheri looked dow
at the girl and asked her what her story was and why was sh
in her room? The girl said she had been assigned to this roo
by the Master-at-Arms and that she had just gotten on the ba
this afternoon. Cheri said under her breath damn! Now I have
deal with another asshole. Cheri didn't say another word to th
girl she just turned around and left the room and walked dow
the hallway and down the stairs leading to the front desk ar
started asking questions of the Master-at-Arms. Why is this gi
in her room? Weren't there any other rooms available? Is anybod
getting discharged soon so this person would have some pla
to go? Her questions were all answered with no, no, no and sh
was told that she would just have to suck it up and deal with th
situation. This was not her private castle it was used by many ar
the girl was one of many.

Cheri was highly disappointed and more than a little perplexe
she was fit to be tied because this girl would not fit in with h
gang. Upon returning to her room, Cheri asked the girl what h
name was and where she was from. The girl said she was fro
Phoenix and her name was Gina Running Eagle, the name caug
Cheri's attention the girl was American Indian so that explaine
her strange looking face. Well maybe she would give her a chan
after all she didn't have much choice right now. Cheri showe
the girl where she could hang up her stuff and told her that th
room was half hers so do not mess with her things, if she wante
to use something or need something ask for it but do not touc
it first. They passed the rest of the evening swapping stories ar
Cheri gave her the rules of the room, you must keep it clean
all costs.

Gina had been on the base for maybe a week or two before e started out on a mission to find herself a husband. Gina said she found an American born man and married him she would t have to go back to the reservation when her tour of duty in e military was up. So every night Gina would go to the Club ming back later and later, sometime she would lie across the d in her uniform because she didn't have time to get undressed d go to bed before she had to report to her job in the morning.

Gina finally latched on to some hick who was coming by the rracks and taking her to the Club and buying her beer all night d then parking with her until the break of dawn. Gina had a ıll yellowish complexion, with jet black stick straight hair that ıs not cut it was chopped up into a terrible bob. Her hair would t curl no matter what she did to it, and they tried everything, ey even tried to put perm in it to no avail. Gina had a boxy squat ;ure that was straight up and down in the back from her neck to r knees. She had slant eyes and a hawk nose and a mouth full ' double crooked teeth.

Gina's hygiene left a lot to be desired, she didn't shower eryday like the rest of them did she would put on her wrinkled ıiform and or her dirty shirt over and over again before washing When Gina would come in from work she would lie down and ke a nap in her uniform. Then when it was time for the Club to ›en she would get up and go to the Club in the same wrinkled ıtfit she had lolled around in. One night Cheri woke up to the d familiar sounds of someone heaving, she laid there quiet for a inute letting the sounds sink in before she realized it was Gina rowing up between her bed and the wall. Cheri jumped up and rned on her light and said get up and get out of my room you ısty filthy bitch.

That night Cheri slept in the TV Lounge on one of the couch
again she was getting sick and tired of this shit. Where did the
bitches come from didn't they have any pride or any self wort
The next day Cheri called the Barracks Chief from her job a
told her what had happened and asked that she find some pla
else for Gina to stay. When Cheri returned to the barracks fro
work that day it was a done deal. Gina was gone, she was mov
to the transient room and she stayed there until she married t
hick she had been working on and put in her requested for
discharge for being pregnant. After those roommates Cheri h
the room all to herself until she got discharged. She was able
have her hen sessions and hold court in her own room and n
offend anyone. Also the majority of the waves were afraid of h
and they didn't want to share her room anyway, not fulltime.

Cheri didn't like things out of place or anyone that drank. S
had an aversion to people who liked alcohol. In her mind on
they got drunk enough they would vomit and she would rather
anything than vomit when she heard somebody heaving it ma
her gag she had a weak stomach and the cleanest room in t
Wave Barracks. Since the Barracks Chief was such a patsy s
was afraid to put anyone in Cheri's room.

Some of the girls in Cheri's clique had suspicions that s
was a CID plant (Criminal Investigations Department). It w
alleged that there was one in every barrack who was the eyes a
ears for the government. Even thought the girls felt she was t
mole they would not come right out and question her for fear s
was the mole. They just felt like there was no way this girl cou
do all the things she did and say all the things she said to hig
officials and get away with it.

If Cheri saw a Commissioned Officer approaching her on the
se to keep from saluting that person she would turn around and
in the other direction or duck into the nearest building. When
e went to the Mess Hall for her meals she wouldn't stand in the
e outside of which she was suppose to do, they went by first
me first served, she said it was too long so she would walk up to
e front door and the silly sailors and marines would salute her
nking she was an officer. She would salute them back and go
o the Mess Hall laughing. Anybody else got wrote up for far
s and would have been placed on restriction. So she had to be
orking for the government. Little did they know that Cheri had
ne through the same process that they had, except she had a lot
heart and people respected people with heart and people who
ok chances. She didn't like saluting people because she didn't
el they were worthy, they weren't any better than she was. So to
ll with paying homage to some asshole that's probably a freak
hind closed doors.

One Monday morning Cheri woke up with a cold and a fever
r throat was so sore she could hardly swallow. Her pajamas and
d linens were damp from her constant sweating all night. She
d been feeling poorly all weekend but today she was really sick,
she did not get up to go to work as usual (in the military you
t up and get dressed and report to work, after roll call you can
l out of line and request to go to sick bay). Cheri just stayed in
d that morning like normal people do when they are sick.

As the Barracks Chief was making her daily rounds f
morning inspection she noticed Cheri's locker doors were st
open for privacy so she peeped in and seeing her in bed she ask
her why she wasn't at work Cheri said because I am sick, I ha
a sore throat, chest congestion and a fever that's why I am still
the bed I don't feel good. The Barracks Chief called sickbay a
had them send over an ambulance to transport her to the ba
infirmary. This was a first! The Chief was beside herself wi
anger she didn't need this confusion first thing Monday morni
no one in her fifteen years of service had just stayed in bed befo
They would have called the Chief or the Base Commander
have somebody else call; this just wasn't done! This was n
protocol! Cheri was taken out of the barracks to the infirmary
ambulance.

Cheri was checked out by one of the doctors and giv
medication to take by mouth for the next few days, she w
transported back to the barracks with instructions that she was
stay in bed for the rest of the week and then report back to wo
the following Monday; the Barracks Chief notified her job of t
situation.

Before noon it had spread all over the base that Cheri h
stayed in bed and refused to go to work and was not being throw
into the Brig or placed on restriction!

She must be the "**Mole**". If anyone else had pulled a stunt li
that they would have been given a Captains Mast and placed
restriction for months, but not Cheri, she got her meals deliver
to her room daily by the Barracks Chief.

The other waves were all pondering the situation and
ıispering amongst themselves why did she get to have her own
om? While the rest of them had to share a room with whomever
e Barracks Chief chose to put with them and they didn't have a
y in the matter. Cheri said and did whatever she felt like doing
d got away with it, something just was not right with this girl,
d she did too many things that were totally out of character
th no consequences. She stood watch (Master-at-Arms)
thout her suit jacket on. She made fun of the girl's names when
e announced their dates over the PA system; she danced in the
ınge. She shot dice in the lounge behind the couches with the
gue marines. Cheri slept on the couch in the lounge when she
ıs suppose to be standing night watch with the excuse that she
ted the 2:00am to 6:30am watch. Cheri would pay people to
ke her watch which they did most of the time, but when she
uldn't find anybody to take her watch and she had to stand
ıtch herself, her excuse for not waking up the people who had
gned the wake-up sheet was because she was sleepy. Some of the
ıves had to be at work early in the morning. So they would sign
e wake-up sheet requesting the different times they needed to
woke up to go to their perspective jobs. Some of them wanted
get up at 5:00am, 6:00am and some as early as 4:00am. When
u stood the Master-at-Arms watch you are suppose to walk the
lls every hour with a flash light, check the entry ways to see that
ey are all secure, then you log the information in the Captains
og and call the Base Commander and tell them who you are and
at Wave Barracks 232 is all secure.

Even though you are suppose to wake people up! Cheri only
oke up half of the people who had signed the wake-up sheet
fore she would fall asleep on the couch herself, you can't wake
ople up if you are asleep yourself. Also when she had the Watch
a girl came back to the barracks intoxicated she would not walk
r to her room, she would tell whoever brought her to the door
just dump the drunken slut in the lounge and she would let
em sleep it off in a chair until the poor girl was able to get up
ıd stagger off to bed.

If Cheri didn't see the roommate of the girl who was drun
she would leave her in the lounge all night and that's where s
would be until late the next morning missing roll call on her jo
When the Barracks Chief came over to start her day, she wou
find the sleeping girl in a chair in the lounge and write her up ar
she would have to attend a Captains Mast (Court Marshall) tha
why they really didn't like her they just pretended that they di
Cheri hated drunks; she felt the girls could go out and should g
out and have fun without getting blotto. In her mind this was
disgrace to the uniform and she was right! What's worst than
staggering disheveled woman in a uniform and high heels. Ar
tricks dealing with circumventing regulations Cheri knew it ar
how to do it. She knew how not to sew her stripes on her unifor
shirts since she was always wearing a jacket she just sewed th
stripes on the jacket sleeve, until one of the blue haired wav
came over impromptu from Menopause Manor while serving
Watch Commander and saw her sitting at the Master-at-Arn
desk without her jacket and noticed she had no stripes on h
shirt. She got off with a warning but was told to have those strip
sewed on by the next day; of which she did.

The only time the blue haired older waves would come over
Barracks 232 was if they had the Watch duty. Most of the old
waves had almost twenty years of service and would be retirir
soon with their pensions for life. So their lives consisted of the
doing their jobs and just trying to finish those last few montl
or years with no "**drama**" they did not want to deal with tho
young wild women, like they hadn't been young once. The old
waves that had husbands lived ashore (off base) in navy housir
or in an apartment in town, so that meant that the ones livir
in Menopause Manor had no man or no permanent man. Th
oldest wave in Barracks 232 was about thirty years old and th
youngest was nineteen.

They had to give Cheri her credit for not many enlisted
rsonnel could go from grade E-1 to E-5 in three years. Cheri
s smart she didn't act the fool all the time she studied and went
to be tested to make a higher rank every chance she got. You
uld only take the test for more rank once a year so when she
ssed the test for E-5 it spread over the base like wildfire. When
u make E-5 you are eligible to move into Menopause Manor
to your own room that came equipped with a real door with a
l lock that locked. No more lockers with open doors for Cheri
e was excited about her pending move. When the senior waves
ard that Cheri had passed the test and made E-5 and would be
gible to move into their quarters with them, they immediately
anged the rules. Having her live with them was not going to fly!
ose women were in a tizzy fluttering around like a bunch of old
ns, holding secret meetings and such until they came up with
idea. They said let her stay in her own room in 232 because
ere are no empty rooms in Menopause Manor.

Truth be told they did not want to be bothered with her and
r bunch, what with all that loud rock and roll music, the loud
lking and laughing and Cheri singing and dancing up and down
e halls; it was too much for them to deal with. At this time in
eir lives those women craved peace and quiet.

Since Cheri had her own room anyway in the underclassmen
rracks she stayed right where she was and everybody was happy,
pecially Cheri. She had always had her own room, because
body wanted to room with her so nothing changed except her
y she made more money and she stayed in her own private room
til she got her discharge.

Chapter Six

Bid Whist Bitches

After living a few weeks in the barracks it became obvio to Cheri that the waves on Treasure Island were like a bag mixed nuts. They all were different and yet they fitted togeth into a very comfortable boring routine they called living. Th would go to their assigned jobs during the day and congrega in the lounge after work until early evening trying to decidir whether or not to go to the Club and dance or just to look. Th time spent in the lounge after dinner was occupied with bid-whi playing, or listening to the community radio or just kibitzing wi some guy who had the nerve to come by the wave barracks ar ask for someone.

The main lounge was for entertaining company, there was tw other lounges located in the living quarter's, one was set up li a theatre for looking at the lone TV and the other had stuff chairs for reading, a pool table, and a ping pong table. When wave has a guest the Master-at-Arms would announce it over t PA system, so and so you have a guest in the lounge. So everybo knew when someone else had company. Normally a bunch girls would come and peek in the lounge, to see who had come see who of the inner circle.

Friday evenings started the marathon bid-whist playing in e lounge from after dinner straight through until Saturday ght. Sometimes they would play straight through until Sunday ening before retiring to their rooms. On those nights of the arathons, some of card players would mix orange pop with wood cohol to get a buzz, one of the girls who worked in the medical partment would have stolen it. It was amazing that they didn't rn out their stomachs.

While the card players held court in a corner of the lounge e non-players such as Cheri, Dora and Angela would dance night to the latest songs on the radio. It would get so loud in e lounge that the other people who weren't in their inner circle ould take their guest and go for a walk in the park or go to the wling alley on base or to the base theatre. After six or seven rls and their guest get together in the lounge it was unreal, some nes they would let the guys play bid-whist too, so they started ming over and just asking for anybody just to get in that lounge. ne main characters that dominated the lounge for card playing re Lara, Tammy, Lois, Cadie, Fanny and Nora.

Nora liked to hold card marathons because her fiancé was t to sea this enabled her to have company and helped with the redom of her life while waiting for her man to return. Treasure land was one of the few military bases that had an abundance black waves. Most bases had a couple but Treasure Island had enty and the black military men would travel from as far away Alameda Naval Air Station, Travis Air Force Base and Moffett eld Naval Air Station to check out the waves on Treasure land. That's why the waves at Treasure Island were so stuck on emselves, they thought everybody wanted them.

Cheri could hang with the best of them, she could talk t slang talk, she was hip to the jive and she carried herself like s had it going on. But she didn't care about these strange peop In her mind she was a leader, she chose to lead and they cho to follow. She believed the world was made up of a whole lot followers and a few leaders. Most people chose to follow becau you don't have to think. To lead you have to be a thinker, you ha to know where you are going and what you want out of life, the girls didn't have a clue. If you don't want anything just follo along and take life as it comes.

It was apparent to the senior waves (grade E-5and E-7) th lived across the compound in "Menopause Manor" who we suppose to be overseeing the junior waves in 232, (Menopau Manor is what Cheri renamed their barracks because they h blue hair and almost twenty or more years of service) who w behind all the shenanigans going on at barracks 232. That gagg of girls kept up a lot of bullshit and the only way you could ke them in their place was through fear, so whoever had the bigge mouth and could cuss the loudest and didn't care if they liv or died ruled the roost. There was only one person who h that much savvy and that was Cheri, Dora was a close secon Cheri ruled those girls like a madam running a whorehouse. T worst perpetrators on the base referred to Cheri as "The Madar because of the control she had over those girls and her leadersh abilities. Those country waves would congregate in her room f hen sessions and lessons on everything from talking to men fashion tips, how to wear their hair, what went with what, th had no style and she did, so they were always trying to borro her clothes.

Cheri was the only one in the barracks that could cut black
ir like a barber or curl hair like a beautician, she would wash
e girl's hair and set it on rollers and when it was dry, comb it out
d style it, those girls started looking pretty good. So the girls
pt coming back to her room looking for her because deep down
side they liked the wildness of Cheri. Cheri kept snacks in her
cker all the time so if she didn't feel like going to the mess hall
she didn't like what they were serving she would have food, it
s little stuff like tuna and crackers, Vienna sausages, cookies of
hich she would share with the others. She had a curling iron and
r own personal radio which was always set on the stations that
ayed the latest music when she was in her room. She smoked in
r room even though it was against the rules.

Cheri loved the military and she was enjoying her tour of
ty to the utmost. She was very patriotic but she had a problem
king orders, which is strange for someone in the military. She
dn't like for people to question her about anything and please
n't ask her why she did something! That was a **no, no**, she
ould snap and go stone crazy asking **WHY? WHY? WHY?** I
d something! If I knew why I did it! I wouldn't have done it in
e first place! I did it because I wanted to! Because I felt like it!
nade a decision and whether it's right or wrong at least I made a
cision and took a stand! What did you do? Nothing! So don't
estion me, who are you to question me.

BID WHIST BITCHES
SUB CHAPTER 6.1

Nora

WHEN NORA WASN'T HOLDING COURT in the lounge playi
cards (bid whist) for hours on end, she could be found sitting
the table in front of the full length mirror in the lavatory area
the first floor shower. She would be equipped with her writi
paper and pens, cigarettes and a bag of hair rollers laughing a
talking and smoking. Always talking to whoever would come
to take a shower or whatever, since this was one of the three plac
you could smoke she took advantage of the time and the space.

Nora was always trying to roll her hair and never doing a ve
good job, because the next day at work she would always have
up in a knot on top of her head. She always had a bunch of whi
girls gathered around her they found her fascinating. She w
considered black but she had real fair skin; as fair as their ow
and her hair was light brown and straight like their own so th
found her exciting to talk to while trying to figure her out.

Nora worked at the Receiving Station in the same office as ıeri, except she was in the back in a secluded glass enclosed :a with Alvarez, they only processed discharge or deployment :ords for Commissioned Officers. It was felt that only someone th a certain kind of quite demeanor and a non-descript look uld be around Commissioned Officers. Being meek and mild ınnered and fair skinned Nora fit the profile for the job of ›rking with officers.

Anyway Nora was a nice country girl from Virginia, she was enty years old, she didn't curse and had no style, nor could she nce but she did smoke a lot, and she had a gold trimmed tooth ;ht in the front.

Nora found Cheri and Dora intriguing, even though the other ıves who had been there longer than the new arrivals; talked out them like they had forked tails because they were so wild. ıe liked the idea that they took chances and didn't care who ln't like it. Nora was always trying to coerce them into teaching r the latest dance steps, they tried but to no avail the girl had o left feet and no rhythm at all. Even though Nora was fair and uld have passed for white at the time, she was not striking in the ›ks department, her figure was fluffy and boxy, she wore black rn rim glasses; and no makeup, not even lipstick to enhance her ›ks.

Nora was slightly knock- kneed and slew footed, and wh
she opened her mouth it was pure country personified. Everyo
liked Nora; she was a real sweet person and a lot of fun to
around, no matter how ridicules someone was, she never has
bad word to say about them at least not that they knew of. No
was using the card games to occupy her time until her boyfrie
Ben came back from overseas, he was on a ship out to sea f
eight months. She felt that if she didn't go to the Club she wou
not be tempted to dance or get familiar with another man out
loneliness. She felt if she didn't go looking for trouble she wou
not get into trouble. So Nora did not go to the Club ever. Wh
Ben returned in seven or eight months they were planning
get married. So aside from playing cards and writing love lette
and going to work she had nothing else going on in her life. B
was madly in love with Nora because she was as close to a whi
woman as he would ever get. Ben being from the south had be
taught that if you are yellow, you are mellow or that the lighter t
skin the better, here he had a woman as fair as any white woma

Back in his hometown he had been afraid to even look up
a white woman, so he felt honored to have his fair fiancé. C
my goodness he had hit the jackpot, he had captured the heart
the perfect girl to take back home to momma. He had the be
of both worlds without offending anyone. So there Nora sat c
Treasure Island like a little hen waiting for the love of her life
return so she could start living.

Bid Whist Bitches
Sub Chapter 6.2

Cadie

ATE WAS A WIZARD WITH a deck of cards she could make em sing in her hands. She could shuffle those cards and make oridge out of them from one hand to the other and she loved to ay bid-whist, there was nothing else she would rather do than ay rise and fly. She was the essence of country girl no drinking smoking or cursing. Cate was so straight that one of the worst rpetrators on the base set his sights on her, he was determined get that girl, he said nobody is that damn good, she is too good be true, and he was going to prove everybody wrong about her; e must have a flaw somewhere in her character there had to be hink in her armor and he intended to find it.

Cate was from some small town in Kentucky; she was real ce and quiet and had a tendency to appear shy. She was short stature abut 5'4" tall, dark skinned with small bones, she had a te heart shaped face and a horrible hair do and a real big butt r her size. Cate was Fanny's roommate. When Cheri arrived the base, Cate had been on the base for a while, she worked in orekeeping and she only had eyes for one man and his name was rri from Indiana. Perri was so dumb he didn't know shit from inola; he was one of the biggest squares on the base this man as lucky to get a date.

When Perri and Cate's relationship hit a rough patch a
they split up to give each other some space, that's when s
started going to the Club with the rest of them and that's wh
Abba who had been lurking in the shadows like a black panth
made his move. It was like watching a deadly snake catching
small helpless mouse. It didn't take much since she had be
dealing with a virtual dead man it was all down hill from the
To Abba, Cate was a challenge to just see if he could pull her fro
her square ass boyfriend, she was definitely not his type, he li
oriental girls.

Abba got real busy wining and dining Cate since he was M
Smooth from Chi Town he felt he had the magic touch wi
women, and he started to work his magic on Cate, whispering
her ear every chance he got telling her how fine she was and ho
good she looked and that she shouldn't be wasting her time wi
Perri, that guy was going nowhere and he could offer her nothin
Why would she want to be tied to some guy who is a looser? Ca
being from so far back in the country that her breathe smelled li
hay had never hear of some of the things he told her he would
to and for her.

He wanted her to be his to come and live with him and
his love; it aroused her interest, she started dating him, "**wro
move**", she was hooked before "**God Got the News**".

Abba Boo Bambini the Third, Son of the first Monte K
the third Majahra and the rightful heir of the Duke of Oxfo
that was the title that he gave to himself, this man was insar
Abba was about 5'7" tall, dark skinned with rose shaded horn ri
glasses. He had a small neat mustache, and keen features. He w
medium built but on the buff side; in today's world he would
considered as dark and swarthy with a sinister look and he talk
a lot of bullshit. Abba could speak some Japanese and Kore
from having been stationed overseas, but on Treasure Island
worked as a Hospital Corpsman. He didn't spend much time
the barracks; he basically lived off base. He would change into h
civilian clothes in the barracks and put his uniform for the ne
day in his briefcase then catch the base bus into San Francisco.

Only a few people knew that Abba was sleeping in town with e Asian girls, he had a fascination and a deep affection for Asian nales.

Since Abba liked to shoot the bull with Cheri, he had told r what was going on with him and that she should keep it to r self because his business was private. One thing Cheri could was keep a secret she didn't reveal any confidences. Abba had ıght her a few phrases in Japanese and he was so impressed th her ability to comprehend the language so quickly that he ought her his basic Japanese book that he had gotten when he ıs stationed in Japan.

Cheri studied it to the point where they would communicate in oanese when they were at work at the theatre, they both worked the base theatre in the evenings and on weekends. They were sponsible for its operation they opened and closed the theatre. ıey ordered and counted the candy, stacked the inventory in e storage room, popped the popcorn and boxed it, prepared the verages, counted the money for the evening filled out the paper ork and made the money drop at the banks night depository ter they closed, they did this seven days a week. Basically they ere running the base theatre for extra money, while they had eir day jobs. Whenever Abba would run into someone he knew the base, he would throw up both of his hands and say "Oh My oul" the man was crazy as a shit house rat.

Sometimes when Abba had something else he wanted to do side work at the theatre he would come over to the Receiving ation and stop by Cheri's desk and ask her in Japanese to work r him that night, he would get a kick out of it when she would ıswer him back correctly in Japanese. Abba did not fool around th the waves on base he said they were too nosey and they lked too much, as I said he got off base as soon as possible every y; until he set his sights on Cate.

Christmas was usually a dismal and lonely time in the barrac
since most of the people would have taken leave and gone hon
or wherever for the holidays. Cheri decided she wanted to sa
her leave and go home when it was warm so she was one of th
few left at the barracks. Since Abba lived mostly off base he w
familiar with the habits of the local people. He knew that it w
at this time of year that people of means would run ads in th
local newspapers looking for someone to house sit for them an
take care of their plants or animals, so that when they returne
home to their house or apartment it would be as they had left
Abba responded to an ad using his most professional manner an
got the job house sitting in the San Francisco Hills.

Since there was only about ten or fifteen people who didn't g
home for the holidays, the word got around that Abba was hou
sitting and having a party; anyone who didn't have a place to g
was invited just bring your own beverages. Cheri and Cate to
one of the guys left on base that had a car so they would have
ride to the party. Abba wanted Cate to come anyway because h
was trying to pursue her in a big way and he had plans for he
That Friday evening they piled into the cars and went into tow
to the address Abba had given to them.

The apartment was very nicely furnished in a cozy kind
way; it was small and very clean with a fire roaring in the fireplac
Abba had put the people's dog in the bathroom. After sittin
around for a while Abba suggested that they go to the store an
get some food, so Cate and Cheri accompanied him to the loc
market where he picked up some beer, Cate suggested that the
should fry some chicken and get some chips and dip.

Once they returned to the apartment, it was implied that ɿeri should do the cooking of the chicken since she was the ıly one who knew how to cook so it would at least be edible. ; the evening wore on more and more people started showing , the word had gotten around all over the base. They brought kinds of liquor and the men started to play cards, some game lled drink or smell, where you had to take a shot if you lost a nd. The females were listening to the radio and talking, since ey didn't have a record player, after all it was someone else's artment and they didn't want to break anything. That little artment was getting smaller and hotter by the minute as Cheri ɔod and fried more and more chicken in that hot oil on that hot ɔve in that hot kitchen; and the body heat of all those people in at tight apartment was adding to the equation and was making e place unbearable.

Cheri was sweating after cooking for hours in that heat, it was ɔwded but they had managed to keep the noise level down so not to alert the neighbors who would have called the police. ıey would have all gone to jail for being in those rich peoples artment. About midnight, Cheri called it a day her legs were tired from standing in front of that hot stove that they were robbing. She said I am done somebody else can take over now, ıd she went into the living room and sank down on the couch, cked off her shoes, she laid her head on her arm which was opped up against the arm of the couch where she immediately ll asleep.

When she woke up it was pitch black and quiet in the room, ing in an unfamiliar place she couldn't make out what was hat or where she was, even though she had not taken a drink of ıything but soda, she still didn't know where she was.

She was disoriented from being so tired, but she knew someo
was lying at the other end of the sofa with her and she did
know who it could be! She started to panic, her heart was raci
she was in a strange place with who knows who sleeping next
her, she told herself to just relax and think. She felt around a
realized she had on all her clothes even her silk stockings, so s
knew her clothing was in tack. The only thing missing was h
shoes and coat.

Since nobody sleeps in their coat she knew that whoever
was down there on the other end of the sofa had not moleste
her. While feeling around in the darkness she felt the person
the other end of the sofa stir, she asked in a soft whisper who
there? The person answered back, it's me Cate, Cheri breath
a sigh of relief she did not want to be caught in a compromisi
position with anybody against her will and since she knew it w
Cate, Cheri curled back up into her position on the couch a
went back to sleep.

Later in the morning when it became light enough to s
her surroundings, she noticed that there were guys asleep at t
kitchen table with their heads resting on their arms and some gu
were on the floor, they were all over the place. Abba said later th
he felt that after that night of drinking it was too dangerous f
them to try to drive back to the base so they had slept wherev
they could. Cate had refused to share the bed with him in t
bedroom, so after fighting him off half the night she had crawl
behind Cheri on the couch. As the day wore on they got up a
straighten the furniture in the apartment and cleaned up the pla
and left to go back to the base, after all there is only so mu
partying a person can stand with that wild man Abba.

The next thing they knew Cate was going out on a regul
basis with Abba and when he got orders to ship out overseas, s
eloped with him and followed him to the Orient Cheri visit
the Bay area a few years later to find that they were back fro
overseas and living in the vicinity, she looked up Cate and pa
her a visit at her home. Cheri was horrified to see the conditi
Cate was in, she was bleary eyed and drinking out of a bottle
liquor that she was carrying around in her purse.

Cheri could not believe this was the same girl. Cate called a ild into the room and introduced her to Cheri as her daughter. was for sure the child did favor her husband but she did not ›k a thing like Cate. Cate saw the questions in Cheri's eyes and .d the girl was adopted by them when they were overseas and at after trying to conceive numerous times, Abba had coerced r to adopt a child under the guise she couldn't have children of r own. Technically that child probably belonged to him and .e of his many chippies.

Anyway Cate appeared to be a very unhappy woman, anybody th half a brain could see and would go to the grave believing at was Abba's child. Cate's unhappiness probably stemmed from e situation; and the drinking was her way of self medicating r taking up with the wrong type of man. Here she was year's er talking crazy and looking wild about the eyes. The child was finitely mixed Black and Japanese but Cate spent zero time renting the child she was relegated to a room in the back of the ›use, it was like she was a visitor in the home you do the math.

BID WHIST BITCHES
SUB CHAPTER 6.3

Tammy

TAMMY, TAMMY, TAMMY.....THIS WOMAN WAS somethi
else, she was twenty years old and quite attractive in a stran
exotic kind of way, she was brown skinned, very shapely and s
kept her hair together in a short feathery style. She wore a l
of makeup she would pile on the pancake makeup, draw on h
eyebrows and put on lipstick and mascara which she applied
night, so she would not have to deal with it in the morning. H
pillow cases were scandalous, especially since they only got cle
linen once a week. Tammy was Dora's roommate.

Tammy had a serious flaw; she had a big gap in her buck teet
right in the front so as long as she kept her mouth closed y
didn't notice it, but when she smiled she kind of reminded you
a rat, of which she had the morals of. Tammy would go out wi
any girl's man in a New York minute and tell them, if they happ
to catch her, that she was doing them a favor! Now you know th
he is a no good cheater. She went with damn near every man
the base behind other people's back.

She started going with her married boss a Sergeant in the :my who was stationed at Treasure Island and worked for the ilitary Police. She went with him for over a year. The man was st as ridicules as she was. The sergeant would take her to his use off base where he lived with his immediate family. He let r spend the weekends lounging around the pool with his wife d young children. He had told his wife that she was his long st cousin that he happen to run into on the base.

Tammy had no morals at all she was like an alley cat and she d not care who didn't like it. The girls use to speculate that ammy might have a mental problem because nobody did the ings she did; she would just throw caution to the wind and do hatever with men. The others would curse and smoke and dance ld but they did not fool around with another woman's husband at was taboo. But Tammy didn't care she said if they can't ep their man that's their problem, they aren't doing something ght. Everybody on base knew of the situation and they told her at what she was doing was some dangerous shit and just plain wdown and that she needed to be more careful and stay out of at woman's house.

She still didn't care, she said if he didn't respect his wife why ould she and all of the nosey people needed to mind their own mn business because she could take care of hers. It came to a ad when they were all invited to a baby shower the Sergeants ife was giving for Fanny at her home.

The Sergeant knew Fanny well since she use to work for him at e Military Police Department along with Tammy before she got scharged. Fanny was married to Dan and had been discharged om the Navy at the time of the shower. That shower was the ost uncomfortable social event those waves had ever been to.

Although the girls were young and inexperienced they cou
still pick up on the fact that the wife suspected something w
going on between her husband and Tammy. She maintained
smiling face and was overly friendly to everyone of the invit
guest except for when she had to speak to or at Tammy then s
had a very cold demeanor towards her. They couldn't wait to g
out of that house, that shower was over so fast it was like it nev
happened; no one wanted to play the games they just nibbled
the food and broke their necks getting out of that house the fi
chance they got.

They were all afraid that the woman would snap at any minu
and pull a gun or a knife and start killing everybody from the ba
thinking they were in on the shit.

The tension was so thick you could cut it with a knife. Anybo
with a brain knew this was a very dangerous situation and th
just wanted to get the hell out of that woman's house, of whi
they did; but Fanny got nice gifts anyway.

Tammy ran around loose on the base for the next two yea
hitting on any new arrival that didn't know her story or her nas
ways, she had to get the fresh meat before they found out she w
crazy. Tammy finally met her match when this big husky 6'6
handsome brown skinned sailor name Eugene arrived on bas
He was assigned to one of the Air Craft Carriers that was dock
at Treasure Island. Tammy was all over Eugene like a dirty shi
She was busier than a one legged man in a butt kicking conte
trying to keep tabs on him and trying to keep the other femal
away from Eugene. Tammy knew how treacherous she could b
when it came down to a man, that's why she was so parano
about Eugene. The crazy part of the whole situation was th
nobody else wanted him but her anyway.

After chasing him for a few months she came up pregnant
d started pressuring Eugene to get married. He refused to
arry her. Everyone on that base knew that if anybody knew
w to protect themselves from getting pregnant it was Tammy
pecially after all the men she had been dealing with, so they
knew she did this on purpose she had a plan to try and hook
ugene. Eugene said he was not marrying anybody because he
asn't ready financially or mentally and he didn't know if the baby
as his or not.

He said he couldn't trust a girl who had slept with him the
st night he met her and knew so many tricks and ways to drive a
an crazy in bed, she didn't learn all that stuff out of some book.

So there was Tammy getting discharged for being pregnant
th no place to go and no one to turn to. Tammy was homeless
til Mia took her into her home. She didn't want to go back to
r family in California with a baby and no husband so she went
d got a job working at a local dairy in the Bay Area. Tammy
orked at the dairy and stayed with Mia for two weeks, sleeping
Mia's couch. Then she left one day while Mia was at work
king most of Mia's clothes with her and without even saying
odbye dog. Tammy was last seen around the Compton area,
here she had come from with her baby boy.

Bid Whist Bitches
Sub Chapter 6.4

Laura

LAURA WAS ONE OF THE oldest waves on the base she w
thirty-two years old from Nut bush, Tenn. She had permane
red eyes and she always looked like she was intoxicated. S
was short in stature and still wore her old lady comfort sho
from boot camp. She had discolored teeth from chain smoki
Chesterfield cigarettes. It came out later that she was intoxicat
most of the time because she kept a bottle of Jack Daniel in h
shoebox, and she would take swigs out it during the day wh
she was in the barracks. If the cravings got too much for her
handle she would come back to the barracks at lunch for a hit.

Laura was Queen of the bid-whist table, they would play nething called rise and fly, which meant when you lost a game u had to get up and somebody else would get to sit down and y until they lost, Laura never got up, she never lost, she would there from Friday evening until Sunday night, chain smoking d dealing those cards and sipping that wood alcohol out of a p can when her regular stash ran out. It was soon common owledge that she was an alcoholic. Laura dated this older short l faced sailor who had been in the Navy for many years, he was ht skin with a multitude of freckles in his face and he had the ne demeanor as she did. He always looked like he was high and also had red eyes.

Since they were both short they made a perfect match. They th always looked disheveled and their navy blues always looked e they needed to go to the cleaners, they always had a lot of lint them and they were just plain dusty looking. Laura was a nice rson but basically distant with people she didn't know well. She ould play cards with the regulars in the lounge, but that was the tent of it.

She did not go to the Club or spend a lot of time talking with e girls, even when she was playing cards she played in a quiet, idious manner, she didn't make small talk and when and if she er lost at rise and fly she would politely gathered her cigarettes d matches and leave the table and the room.

Cheri would talk at Laura just to see if she could get a nversation out of her. Laura would answer the questions but ver volunteer any extra dialogue, this intrigued Cheri since she d never met a stranger unless she didn't want to be bothered, she worked on Laura until she got into her good graces. Laura ought Cheri was quite different from the other girls so she rmed up to her to such a degree, that Cheri was allowed to sit Laura in her room. Normally Laura didn't want other people her room, just her and her roommate.

Laura's roommate was a real odd ball character, she was feet tall and bone thin for her height, and her skin was so yell that she looked like she had jaundice. This roommate didn't wa anybody in that room but her and Laura either, because she did want her secret getting out, that she was a bed wetter and she w also a closet drunk. Laura told Cheri that the woman washed h sheets herself every evening in the laundry room, and had ev went into town and purchased extra sets of sheets of her own. T roommate was perfect for Laura because they both drank, the g would drink herself into a comma every night and then wet t bed, so to avoid sleeping on those pissy sheets and stinking up t room she would do her own laundry every evening and be able change the bed daily with the extra sheets. It wasn't mandato that you use the navy linen you could if you felt like it purcha your own.

Cheri didn't understand how she had gotten away with bei a bed wetter for so long, because the girl had previously been the Army for two years before joining the Navy. Since Laura h let Cheri into her world even going so far as to introduce h to her main man and offered Cheri some of her stash of alcoh that's how Cheri knew that Laura was drinking a lot.

Laura asked Cheri if she wanted to go to a Rock and R Concert with her and her man the upcoming weekend, she h gotten the tickets for free because she knew some of the peop that were part of the entertainment. Cheri said sure she did have anything else to do, so they went to the Cow Palace to s Laura's cousin sing.

The top billing for the show was some group name James
rown and the Flaming Flames, and then some other local groups
ng, when Laura's cousin finally came out she was just some
inny brown skinned woman with real short hair, who was with a
l skinny dark skinned man who played the guitar, they sounded
etty good but Cheri couldn't get into the groove of the concert
cause they had to stand up there were no seats and there was
wdust and straw on the floor and she was tired of standing up.
later came out the girl was named Annie Mae Bullock and the
an was Ike Turner, Laura's cousin was Tina Turner. They didn't
ay to mingle with the entertainment after the show, since Laura
as pretty tanked up and Cheri had never been that impressed by
ople who were not famous.

Laura and Cheri hung around together for a while and then
ey parted ways, since they really didn't have anything in common.
aura might have gotten transferred to another base, it was not
portant people came and people went.

BID WHIST BITCHES
SUB CHAPTER 6.5

Dora

DORA WAS ONE STRANGE LOOKING female. She was skinı with extremely bow legs and large feet. She was about 5'4" t: but if her legs had been straight she would have been 5'6" or mo: She was twenty-one and she was full grown, she could buy alcoh which she loved dearly. Dora was totally devoid of any brea tissue her chest was as flat as a man's. She had big pop eyes aı a wide juicy mouth with a gap in her front teeth and one of tl front teeth was covered in gold, she had an enormous black mo right between her eyes, it was so big it looked like a growth. Do had a head full of thick wooly hair which she chopped off herse so it was long on the top and real short on the sides and in tl back, she looked like a walking mop about the head.

Dora had an extremely filthy mouth and she got a kick out saying filthy things to shock people while grinning and watchiı their faces. She was not friendly with most of the girls she kind hung around the outskirts of the circle of friends Cheri had mad Dora performed scandalous dances at the Club and she treat men terrible. She was harder on a man than the Chain Gan but guys always took to her for that bad treatment, it just goes show, the worst you treat a man the better they like it.

Dora was real brainy she had passed the Radioman Test with
-ing colors, so she worked at the Radio Control Tower listening
all those dots and dashes, she could decipher that stuff like a
eeze. That was the job Cheri had wanted but she didn't pass
e test. Dora also got to work at night and sleep all day in the
rracks. She made extra money because that job was one of the
ghest paying jobs the Navy had for enlisted personnel, and they
so got paid some kind of incentive pay for being up all night.

She only had to work three or four nights out of the week, the
st of the week was her own free time that she could do with as
e wished. That's how she was able to get into all kinds of devious
uff she had too much free time. Dora had started dating a fat
ilor she had met at the Club. He was giving her money so she
arted buying some cheap clothes in town. He would bring her
nts of liquor, the brand she liked so she was always tipsy. At first
ora said she was not putting out to him, but she was. After she
t drunk one night she told on herself. That man use to follow
r around the base crying real tears because she wouldn't give
m the time of day unless she felt like it (she was a dominatrix
fore they discovered the term). It came out later that the man
as married with a wife and kids back in San Diego.

So whatever Dora was putting on his ass; he had it coming
r cheating on his wife they didn't feel sorry for him. Dora and
heri got along pretty good for a while at first until Cheri figured
t what kind of person Dora really was and decided she didn't
ant to be associated with her. They were like beauty and the
ast, but they both could cuss like sailors.

In the beginning of their friendship Dora would come in from
r late night dates with the fat sailor and wake Cheri up in the
iddle of the night to give her a blow by blow detailing of her
ening. Telling her where she had been that night and what she
ade him do, she would be half drunk with her pop eyes red from
inking and her wide mouth would be bubbling saliva out of the
rners and she would get right down in Cheri's face since she
ould be in the bed and her breathe smelled like she had smoked
whole carton of cigarettes and drank a fifth of whatever.

At these times Cheri wanted to take something and kno
Dora's drunken head off because she would have fallen asleep f
the night and here comes this nut waking her up, when she h
to get up at 6:00am to go to work and besides she didn't real
care what this creature did or didn't do, she needed her slee
She couldn't understand why Dora clung to her the way she d
anyway, they weren't that close any more. Cheri didn't trust Do
anymore her radar told her to get space and distance betwe
them, of which she did. Cheri would greet the other girls by sayi
hey what's happening? Dora would say "Hey Motherfucker" ai
laugh at the shock and distaste on their faces.

In the beginning they had created new dances together ai
had tried them out at the Club but that was then and this is no
people out grow folks and move on. Cheri didn't want to
bothered with Dora period. Before when they operated as a tea
because they didn't know anybody else, some of the waves we
afraid of them, but since then Cheri had made friends with t
other girls and they knew she was just some crazy wild girl havi
fun and the guys loved her. Cheri had said she didn't come in
the navy looking for a home, she had a home, and the only m
she could take home was a Brigadier General, so those low lev
enlisted men knew they didn't stand a chance with her with the
$40.00 every two week asses.

Dora had a lot of shit going on on the side that the others kne
nothing about including her ex-friend Cheri. She had become re
secretive and sneaky or maybe it was her guilty conscious getti
the best of her. She became very paranoid and jumpy when sh
was around them which wasn't often since she was living off ba
by this time, she was sharing an apartment with a little beatn
guy named Niles.

Niles also worked at the radio tower. The guy later became a's husband (Bea the girl from Miami). Dora used him to get r females, because Niles was a good-looking guy he and Dora ould go out to the local clubs together in San Francisco and he ould buy drinks for the loose women he would pick up with ora's money, he would make all the right moves on the girls like was really getting into them and get them to go back to the artment they shared. Where he would continue to ply them th drinks until they didn't know what was going on or cared at at point and then Dora would have sex with them while they re basically out of it. This all came out in the wash after she nt crazy in the barracks.

Dora had also made friends with a bunch of thrill freaks she t in the city. They were suppose to be school teachers that lived the same apartment building as she did. These freaks would ve parties on Sunday afternoons or on Monday evenings, now body in their right mind has a party on Sunday or Monday. Dora ould round up as many of the waves on the base as she could to e back into town to the parties. They couldn't figure out what e was getting out of bringing those girls to those parties maybe e was getting paid, they didn't know, but she continued to do it e it was her job until she went crazy. Dora only took Cheri once a Sunday afternoon, then her new friends pulled her aside and ld her not to bring that girl back since she didn't drink they dn't think she was much fun, they felt she was a drag. By this ne Dora and Cheri had grown apart anyway they had nothing common except they were both females.

Dora had developed a real bad habit of coming on the ba
in the daytime while the girls were at work, and going throu
Cheri's things and taking her suits and jewelry and wearing the
when she felt like it and getting them dirty and full of wrinkl
with out Cheri's permission. Cheri did not like people goi
through her personal things period and to take them with o
asking that was the end of their relationship. Cheri had gott
tired of the Club scene and got her self a part-time job at t
base Theatre it occupied her spare time so she didn't have tin
for those parties anyway. It became obvious to everybody wh
was going on at those freak sessions, a lot of drinking and pairi
off. Tammy loved going to the parties a lot! Because she liked
drink and she was a thrill freak, it got so good to her; she start
missing roll call at work on Mondays. When Tammy did sho
up for morning roll call one Monday afternoon, she was put
base restriction; she could only leave the barracks to go to wo
and to the mess hall for thirty days. It was all over the base
that evening that she got hung up with the drinks and had h
sex with Dora.

By this time Dora was living a strange and wild life style doi
a lot of drinking and drugs. The word had gotten back to the ba
about her actions and the crowd she was hanging out with. Do
went crazy in the barracks one Monday evening, when she w
there to take her scheduled turn standing duty as the Master-a
Arms. She started running up and down the hallways screami
at the top of her lungs that she was not going to let them put th
big black dick in her.

The Barracks Chief was called by the Master-at-Arms on du
at the time; the Master-at-Arms was waiting for Dora to relie
her. The Barracks Chief walked over to 232, she didn't know wh
to expect from those girls and was totally out of her eleme
having to deal with this crazy, black, ugly woman running arou
making such a derogatory statement.

After the Chief analyzed the situation she called the Base ommander and told him what she thought the problem was. The ommander in turn sent the Medics over to the barracks. Dora s placed in restraints and she was transferred immediately to aknole Naval Hospital to the psychiatric ward. Bea and Cheri nt to visit Dora a couple of weeks later at the hospital, and she s so paranoid it was a shame. Dora was balled up in a small ot with her skinny arms wrapped around her skinny legs in a erstuffed arm chair; starring at them with her big vacant pop es and when she did speak she asked them what they wanted?

Looking from one to the other she directed her next question Bea; she looked directly at her and said why did you bring r? She pointed at Cheri with her skinny dry finger, which rely needed some lotion or something on it. When she turned r head in Cheri's direction Cheri noticed she was looking real ange like she was waiting for the other shoe to drop or she was ticipating something to happen. Dora was starting to freak out badly that she started to tremble and her breathing was getting ıder by the minute, her skinny chest heaved in and out, the ins in her neck were prominent and her fists were balled up like e was filled with an inner rage and wanted to hit something or mebody.

So Bea and Cheri mumbled their goodbyes but Dora did not spond, she didn't even grunt when they left. Dora stayed in the ospital for another six weeks for observation and was given a edical discharge or so they heard. As they say what goes on in e dark will come to the light. All her chickens had come home roost at once, so to speak.

The bitch had always been crazy, a drunk and a bi-sexual they st didn't know it. It must have really taken a toll on Dora keeping that stuff hidden inside, all that malicious deceit bottled up side. Using drugs and not getting the proper rest or food just rew her over the edge and they had thought she was a lot of fun. also came out that Dora was the barracks thief she was robbing y and everybody to buy drugs and alcohol and women.

Since there were no locks on the lockers or the dresser drawe in their rooms they had no place to lock up their valuables everybody was a target, especially when you went to the show Dora would creep into the different rooms and go through the lockers and their purses and take all their money she would leave them none. She was almost like a pirate coming into t barracks while they were all at work and going through the things taking whatever booty she found to her liken.

This bitch was 100% no damn good, not one of them w making as much money as she was, since she made extra mon being a radioman and making night differential. The last th heard she was back where she came from getting a check fro the government for being an asshole, and the stealing abrupt stopped as soon as she left so case closed. After she was gone later came out she had made a subtle advance on Fanny. On when Fanny was looking for Tammy she broke through the lock doors into the room to find Dora standing there naked as a jaybi fresh from the shower, when she saw it was Fanny she flashed h a gold toothed smile and lifted her skinny arms over her head ar standing there in all her glory, she said you better knock befo you come in here or you might see something you might like.

Fanny burst out laughing as she turned and made her ex from the room, like somebody, anybody who wasn't blind, cripp or crazy would be attracted to that horrible creature, Cheri ha only befriended her because she felt sorry for her.

Bid Whist Bitches
Sub Chapter 6.6

May

AY THE ALLIGATOR GIRL, THIS girl was one fine mess (she
s Bea's roommate). Cheri had never in her life, seen such a
entally screwed up individual walking and talking and taking
urishment by mouth. This girl would go to work and come
aight back to the barracks and read Nightstand Books over and
er again while lying in bed. She kept a stash of tuna fish and
ackers, and other assorted junk food in her locker so she didn't
ve to waste time going over to the mess hall to eat. Periodically
ey would see her coming from or going to the shower. Bea and
heri use to laugh their asses off over her antics. May befriended
heri because Cheri told her one day that she needed to go get
r hair done properly. She told her that her hair style was not
to par and she needed to put on some makeup and just fix
rself up. May started going into town to the Hairdresser with
heri but that was as far as she would go. She wasn't interested
makeup or hanging out at the Club or interested in what was
ing on in town just her books. Bea and Cheri said to each other
hat's the point she's only laying in bed reading those filthy books
e had no visitors and no dates.

She was strictly a loner. May was tall about 5'10" and weigh
about 160 lbs which was big in those days, she was twenty yea
old from Ohio.

May had big bulging eyes and everyday was a bad hair d
for her until Cheri turned her on to the beautician in tow
May had a space between every tooth in that real wide mou
which reminded Cheri of an alligator. Her social life consist
solely of those books she would read, and they were so filthy th
would make you ashamed to be caught reading them. She wou
say you can read one but give it back because I want to read
again.........

May never went to the Club; she was afraid of men, real me
She didn't have a problem with her fantasy fellows in the boo
Cheri introduced her to the base dork to get rid of him (she h
got tired of using him. For a month she had gone out with hi
along with her friend Bea, she refused to go out with him alo
and he was so desperate that he accepted the dates on any tern
Cheri had been driving his car all over the base even though s
had no license). This man couldn't buy a woman, he was so squa
it made no sense Cheri use to wonder to herself how a pers
could be so dumb and live that's why she felt May and him wou
make a great couple.

Clyde was not bad looking from the neck up, he was fair sk
with hazel colored eyes a cute mouth but that's where it ende
He had a boxy squat shaped body with a extremely high ass ar
knock knees so bad it looked he was walking on stilts. Aft
Cheri introduced them theirs was a match made in heaven th
had so much in common like pent up sexual frustration, May ar
Clyde dated for one month and they were so into each other th
they couldn't take it another day so they went and got married
City Hall one Monday and moved immediately into any availab
Naval Housing.

So May finally got to put into practice all that pent up sexual ıstration from her readings and she had a great partner what th his unfulfilled fantasies. Everybody on base was making ts because they knew that they had to have an outrageous sex e. They only came out of their Navy housing to go to work d get food. May got so busy doing the horizontal mambo that e got pregnant the first month of her marriage. When she got ;charged the following month, she was happy as a lark to be le to spend all her free time servicing her new husband.

In those days if a female got pregnant she was automatically ;charged even if she was married, you were gone as soon as they uld type up your papers. It seemed that those girls sole purpose r joining the Navy was to find a husband. They would hone on some poor lonely fool, his first time away from home and thin two to three weeks they were getting married.

They would rush to the base chapel in their rented wedding wns; yes they rented gowns in San Francisco by the hour. They uld get a solid gold band at the Commissary for fifteen dollars it was on. The marriage situation got so bad and out of hand at the government passed a rule. Even if you got married and t pregnant you had to stay at least six months. The government ıs loosing money what with outfitting, training and feeding and ing teeth on those miserable waves they were not getting their oneys worth. Uncle Sam was paying to ship them all over the untry after training them and their only mission was to get me young clodhopper to the alter, him being sexually frustrated didn't take much and the government was being played the ol.

Bid Whist Bitches
Sub Chapter 6.7

Angela

Angela was from upstate New Jersey. She was about 5'
tall with light Carmel colored skin and light brown eyes. Sh
had medium length brown hair and a good figure, with nice leg
Angela had a wide pink mouth and big feet of which she was se
conscious of, she was twenty years old. Angela didn't wear mak
up and the guys thought she was sharp until they got to know h
better. The men felt that by her being from New Jersey she had
going on. Little did they know that the woman had very very lo
self-esteem; she would fuck a doorknob if that was all she cou
get her hands on at the moment.

Angela got a job on base as a storekeeper so she worked wi
and around a lot of men checking in and store housing supplie
Damn near all those men got to know her intimately. Angela w
a freak from way back she was a person who couldn't control h
emotions she kept it hidden as best she could. When you first m
her you would think she was just a dumb dork because she alwa
acted so oblivious to what was going on, like people's actions an
the way they portrayed themselves didn't matter to her.

She was fascinated by Cheri and Dora, but then who wouldn't ? Cheri was everything she was not, and Dora was so out of ntrol that it was unbelievable. Angela took to emulating Cheri; e tried to dress like her and say slang things like she did, they ould hang out together on the base, going to the Mess Hall and e Club, or to the Theatre or the Bowling alley. They would even into town shopping together to get outfits to wear to the Club. ecause Cheri was familiar with all the regular guys, Angela use tell Cheri which ever guy she didn't want to give him to her, e wasn't picky but Cheri was; so she knew she would only be tting the best of the best even if they were leftovers.

The guys hung around Cheri, because she was fun and would y or do whatever she wanted to, whenever she wanted to she as not looking for a husband. She was not a threat; she wasn't asing that little gold ring she was just out to have a good time. ost of the guys were not looking for a wife they were just being ld and free also. Whenever Cheri introduced Angela to some the guy at the Club she would always go and act crazy, doing umb stuff like, standing in the middle of an open field on base th whoever wanted to walk her back to the barracks kissing and y humping. This kind of behavior does not make you unpopular nong the base freaks but what about when you want people to ke you serious. As far as the few normal people on base were ncerned, her reputation was shot all to hell.

Angela had a real bad habit of having sex with total strange
Once after she had been on the base for a while; the girls we
going to a private party in town, and asked her if she want
to come along because she was just sitting in the lounge doi
nothing on a Saturday night. Once she got to the party she start
grinning and talking with some strange man that was at the par
After a period of time Cheri asked to use the bathroom, she w
told by the host to go down the hall and make a right of which s
did and not knowing the layout of the house she opened a do
and came face to face with Angela intertwined with the stran
man dancing in the nude in a room that was only lit by a nig
light; Angela let out a little gasp and dropped down to the flo
while trying to shield her small breast with her arms, Cheri was
shocked at what she had walked in on, it took a moment for her
regained her composure enough to mumbled excuse me.

Then she turned around and closed the door behind her ar
went back to the party not even using the facilities. Cheri was
traumatized she didn't have to use the bathroom. All she want
to do was leave that party and go back to the safe haven of t
base. Nobody knew what kind of birth control Angela was
she never got pregnant, it was later revealed that she couldn't ha
children anyway. She would go behind the other girl's backs ar
have sex with their boyfriends, plus she told lies to make hers
look better than she was.

Dancing and smiling that was Angela's fortay, and when s
smiled her top teeth fit perfectly on to her bottom teeth, ar
it resembled the joker except she had a small gap in the fro
of her teeth. Her teeth were clean and that was a good thir
because if you are going to smile all the time at least have go
clean teeth. The other waves in the barracks use to wonder wh
Angela's story was, because she would shower constantly in t
morning and at night. Whatever clothes Angela had worn th
day had to be washed that night before she went to bed. Ange
was such a washing freak that she would clean out Cheri's laund
bag without being asked.

Angela would wash Cheri's dirty clothes while she was in wn having fun spending the weekend with her friends. It was t unusual for Cheri to come back to the barracks Sunday night ter having been away for the weekend and find her laundry g cleaned out by Angela, and her clothes all washed and put vay. Cheri felt a little uneasy about somebody else handling her rsonal things but she didn't complain because she had clean othes when she got back. Most of the girls did their laundry ce a week because that's all that is necessary.

Since you had more than one set of underwear and your iforms had to be dry cleaned; unless it was summer then you ore your light blues and they were made out of some kind of acron material that could be washed and ironed; so the only iled things would be your underwear and your white shirts and ockings.

It came out later that the bitch had a filthy mind, so she became compulsive bather to try to over compensate for her thinking. ngela bathed so much that she developed a body rash so sever at she went to the infirmary to find out what the problem was, ice she couldn't stop itching and scaling skin was flaking off of r. She was told that she had to stop bathing two or three times day because she was drying out all her skins natural oils. She as given some creams to use but she didn't stop she kept right n bathing.

The reason Angela was so easy with men was that she never uld achieved an orgasm while having sex. She was chasing at illusive orgasm searching for the release she could never em to achieve because she was not being true to herself, and e was not real she was a plastic phony person who didn't think e was good enough. In today's world she would be considered nymphomaniac, because of all the partners she had. None of r relationships ever lasted, the guys felt like they were doing mething wrong because they couldn't satisfy her so they would arted feeling inadequate and uneasy being around her when she ouldn't have been having sex with them in the first place.

You can be too easy, then people get leery of you wonderi
what's wrong with that girl, you don't even have to buy her a gi
or take her anywhere special and it's all laid out for you, that w
Angela.

She didn't play cards much she preferred to listen to the mus
and try to dance. Angela loved to dance, she was always twisti
and gyrating to some kind of music, the only problem was she h
no rhythm. Men would get the wrong impression of her thinki
she was a sexpot and was shaking it up for them, trying to enti
them by showing them how she could move. It was sad to wat
but aside from her being queen of the freaks she was ok in h
place. You just couldn't trust her because as soon as she was ab
she would stab you in the back and tell you man or whoever yo
were seeing at the moment some bullshit, trying to sabotage yo
relationship because hers was in the toilet..

Bid Whist Bitches
Chapter 6.8

Lois

ʟ Lois with the tiny little voice was the height of mininity or so she thought. She was short only about 5'2" tall .d very petite, Lois was twenty one years old. Lois always wore ree or four inch high heel shoes at all times to compensate for r height. She was light brown skinned with shoulder length .ir, she had small features and if her disposition had been better e would have reminded you of a living doll. Lois' physical flaws :re she was extremely knocked kneeded and pigeon toed. Lois ıs from a small town in Georgia so she spoke with a deep drawl .d she would really lay it on thick when she was around a man. ; tiny and cute as she was this girl invented the word freak. She .d this boyfriend, a marine name Rufus who suffered from the apoleon Complex because he was short for a man and very dark. e swaggered when he walked with his arms held out at his sides :e he was "**The Shit**" and since he worked for the base Police epartment he thought he was invincible. Nobody liked Rufus ıt Lois, the other marines on base couldn't stand him they knew : had a wife and kids in southern California.

Most of the marines on base knew Rufus was just using Lo
for sex until he could get back to his family. She thought he w
madly in love with her and was going to marry her when he g
his discharge in the next six months. Lois and Rufus would e
each other up it was almost cannibalistic to watch if you happe
to be in the car with them, at every stop sign or red light anytin
the car was stationary for more then a minute it was on; he wou
have his tongue down her throat and his hand up her skirt it w
embarrassing. They were known as the two dogs by everybody
the inner circle on the Base.

One Saturday night most of the base gang was attending
house party in Berkeley given by one of the interns at the UCL
Medical Center, when Lois and Rufus showed up, they peruse
the premises then asked the host, a person they did not kno
personally, if there was a bedroom they could use! Here's a hou
full of people from different walks of life socializing and th
come in and ask to get busy. The host looked a little perplexe
but said ok and showed them to a room; but he soon spread th
word about what was going on to everybody that was there.

Upon exiting the bedroom, Lois had the nerve to ask the lac
of the house if she had a douche bag she could use! Those peop
were appalled. Lois had no shame where Rufus was concerne
she did whatever he wanted whenever he wanted; she was lil
his sex slave and the man was not even handsome. So everyboc
on base wondered what was the connection, why was she
awe of this short, ugly man that looked like a troll in a uniforr
Sometimes when they were having their hen sessions in Cher
room, Lois would get silly and tell some of the girls what he w
doing to her. It came out that the man had a magic tongue th
she couldn't resist. Lois said it was worth it, whether she w
talked about or not because Rufus could do more with his tongu
than "Chef Bor R Dee" could with a meatball.

Lois said just thinking about him and what he was going to to her made her moist; and when he was on duty and couldn't t away she would just think about him and have an orgasm. ıfus was short for a man only about 5'5" tall but he was carrying ›ig stick that hit Lois's g-spot every time they got together and you listened closely she said you could hear her screaming for iles.

The girls would all burst out laughing at the things she said cause of course no one really believed her, except Tammy, she ıs a thrill freak herself and had formulated a mental rolodex in r head; in which she at that very moment Lois was boasting out Rufus' prowess in the bedroom, Tammy was casting her es around the room scoping out the expressions on the other rls faces, meanwhile filing the material in her brain to check out ıfus the first chance she got; which didn't take long since she ›rked at the Military Police Department also.

Rufus used Lois until he got his discharge and slipped away ıder the cover of darkness never to be seen or heard from again. ıe was crushed for months. She couldn't sleep or eat and was osing weight she couldn't afford to lose, and she kept asking erybody she came in contact with that she though might have ıown him did they know how to get in touch with him. Lois ıllowed in self pity for the next several months, when she couldn't ke it any more she started going out with one of the worst rpetrators in the military a guy named Herman. He wanted be called H-Baby from the "D" short for Detroit she was so sperate and hard up for a man that she got all into him in a ısh. He was stone crazy and he was not good looking, he had a rge juicy mouth and talked a lot of crap, but he had a car which ıabled them to get off base and hole up in the local motels.

Apparently he was laying it on her ass because she came to heri a few months after they had met and told her she was going marry Herman and asked her to be her maid of honor Cheri id yes, why not she had never been in a wedding before.

Lois and Cheri went dress shopping they found a real ni
wedding dress for Lois, it was a last year sample but because Lo
was so small in stature she was able to get the dress for little
nothing. Cheri spent more on her dress that the bride and then s
had to find shoes and get them dyed to match, but they manag
to get it all together for the big night. They had two weeks to p
the wedding together and it was suppose to go off smoothly b
there was quite a few hitches.

The hall cancelled on them because H-Baby couldn't come
with the deposit and they had to use a house that belonged to
homosexual man that H-Baby knew. While the girls were upstai
getting dressed to march downstairs in front of the minister a
the waiting guest for the ceremony, which consisted mostly of t
regulars from the base, H-Baby arrived empty handed. He did n
have the flowers for the girls to carry. He had forgotten to ord
the flowers; the girls were upstairs in a tizzy they didn't kno
what to do, how can they walk down the aisle empty handed? S
one of the guests went to the neighborhood florist and boug
all of what they had left on Saturday night before closing, whi
consisted of three corsages and they broke them apart and carri
them as a bouquet which looked really cheap and shabby. But t
worst part was there were no beverages to serve the guests. T
groom said don't worry about it and he passed the hat to colle
enough money to go and buy a bottle of Vodka and a cheap bott
of Bourbon to compliment the lunch meat sandwiches they we
serving along with the cake. They should have gone to City H
and got married, if you can't afford a wedding why do it? There w
no decent food and no music except for records and no beverag
and the groom was broke so what was the point.

Lois was embarrassed but she quickly got over it, she didn't
lly care she was getting married. She would have a husband
en if he was not up to par. And she was getting a set of rings
th a diamond the size of a pin head. Those rings couldn't have
st more than a hundred dollars tops. Lois should have ran from
at place and not looked back, but no she refused to be out done
she married the fool. They moved into an apartment with
other couple because he couldn't afford the rent by himself and
e applied for discharge from the Navy, with the high hopes
finding a good civilian clerical job that paid real money and
at was the end of Lois. They had a child and she followed
m around until he got discharged and they set up housekeeping
gether in Detroit city.

CHAPTER 7

Beatrice

MS. BEATRICE JACKSON BETTER KNOWN as Bea; w considered the classy vampire of the group because she had sha pointed white teeth. Bea had a cute figure once you got past h high pockets. She wore her hair short but hanging long over h right eye she was twenty-two years old. Bea had a light brov body and a high yellow heart shaped face it probably came fro having skin treatments. She said she had suffered with acne a teenager although I didn't understand how that was possible sexually active as she was; this girl was getting more sex than t average married woman. Bea was sweet and she had a good hea which is surprising for someone from Missouri. Cheri met B in the Receiving Station where she also worked as a typist in t typing pool. One morning at work Cheri happen to look up fro her typing to see Bea standing and talking with the sailor who desk was in front of her own. As she continued to look she notic there were streams of blood running down Bea's legs; Cheri g up from her desk and walked over to stand behind her and said a whisper in her ear "walk in front of me to the restroom" nobo noticed the two of them leaving the big barn like office, once the bathroom Bea cleaned herself up and was forever grateful Cheri; since she was in the process of aborting a baby.

What a way to make a friend. After Bea passed the fetus
d felt it was safe enough to go over to the medical department
mplaining of heavy bleeding she was sent to Oaknole Navy
ospital for a D&C. A week later she was back on the job at the
ceiving Station and Bea and Cheri remained friends until Bea
t discharged and moved away. Bea had been on the base a long
ne when Cheri arrived, in fact she didn't have that much time
t to serve.

Bea was famous for sneaking into the Marine barracks after
urs to sleep with her boyfriend who was the marine that had
ocked her up. How she accomplished that feat was beyond the
pe of reason of the others on base, since there was someone
duty at the front desk around the clock. It was rumored that
marine boyfriend was good friends with all the other marines
d they would look the other way when he wanted to sneak
r in and have company for the night. Bea also liked to go out
th the older civilian men that worked on the military base in
ferent government capacities. One of her many male friends
no worked as the Manager of the Mess Hall let Bea and Cheri
ve his car one Saturday afternoon while he finished working
shift.

Neither one of those girls was qualified to drive or had a valid
iver's license. Cheri was familiar with cars because she had
iven other guy's cars many times previous, but she didn't have a
ense so technically she could not drive. Bea wasn't even familiar
th the handling of a car other than riding in one. This man was
arried with children and lived in Oakland he was established,
t he gave no thought to the idea of what if they have an accident
th the car? How could he explain it to his wife? Bea and Cheri
ought the man was just plain crazy to let them have his new car
afternoon but they took it and they were driving all over the
vy base in his car until Cheri who was the driver, got tired and
red and they decided to take his car back to him.

Another older civilian male friend of Bea's took them in
San Francisco one Saturday night to an upscale night club call
the "Moulin Rouge" the place was dimly lit and very crowded a
smoke filled, aside from the two of them there was hardly a
other female patrons just a room full of men.

After they had been escorted to their table by the hostess a
their drink order was taken, the Master of Ceremonies announc
the name of some female that was coming out to do her act
striptease. The band started playing and the place fell silent all ey
were riveted on the stage, the girls stopped chattering among
themselves and turned and stared as this lovely young wom
strolled out onto the well lit raised stage. She did a fantastic str
tease; this was a first for Cheri and Bea they had never been
a strip tease before, they thought they were being taken to sor
regular night club, the man never mentioned it was a striptea
joint.

The tall willowy shaped dancer started gyrating wh
removing her long black satin gloves and her skin tight black flo
length gown and when she had finished her routine to the lo
thumping music and wolf whistles; she had taking off all of h
clothes down to a g-string and pasties. The pasties on her brea
had tassels on them and she could manipulated her breast in su
a way that the tassels swirled in different directions at the sa
time. Bea and Cheri looked at each other and burst out laughi
they thought this was amazing the way she could maneuver h
body, other than that they were not impressed by the place or t
girl. Bea and Cheri were more amused by their ridiculous da
they were so busy laughing at him, because he kept drinking o
of his own private stash of some kind of liquor called Aniset
or something like that. He had been drinking it since they le
the base and all the way over to the Club in San Francisco. Aft
they had been seated and the waitress asked what they wanted
drink, he had ordered the same thing.

Bea and Cheri were not drinkers so they order a Tom Collins a Vodka Collins and sipped off of it the entire night. They ought their date was a complete fool to drink the same stuff night and then order and pay for what he already had in his sk in his cars glove compartment. The best part of the night for em was laughing at him, and he was so stupid he didn't know hat they were laughing so much about but he would join in henever they started laughing. He just thought they were two ry attractive cheap dates because he'd only had to buy them one ink each.

Bea was famous for rounding up some old guy to take her d Cheri out on dates on the weekend because she was more phisticated in that arena, she knew how to tease the men and ake them think they stood a chance with her, but they always ent out as a team so the guy couldn't get fresh, then they would ugh about it until Bea found the next sucker.

Bea served the rest of her time and in the eleventh hour arried the Beatnik type guy named Niles that had shared an artment with Dora they eloped to Reno one weekend. Bea ally kept that relationship on the Q.T. no one knew they were en dating, not even Cheri her supposedly best friend. When ey heard she had married Niles, Bea was the talk of the barracks r weeks. They got a cute furnished apartment in San Francisco d set up housekeeping and put their marriage license in a frame the wall in their living room. I guess they wanted everybody know that theirs was a real marriage they were legal and that ey were not just shacking up. After Niles served the rest of his ur of duty and got his discharge, he applied and was accepted Air Traffic Controllers School and they moved away to some ace in Texas.

Bea's new husband was a little handsome guy with a messed mentality about life and drugs, but he thought the sun rose d set in Bea's ass. I guess if you are going to marry someone at ast let him idolize you so kudos to Bea.

CHAPTER 8

Mia

MIA, IF YOU REMEMBER WAS the barracks bully until Che
arrived on the scene. She was very nice looking and she kne
it. She was brown skin, very tall and big boned, she had should
length hair and doe shaped eyes, and a mega watt smile. M
was a size twelve or fourteen and she was getting married in
few weeks because she had gotten pregnant(again) by her prese
boyfriend a little nerd of a guy named Buck who wore bla
horn rimmed glasses, he worked in the medical department as a
X-Ray Technician for the Navy.

When Mia arrived at the base she was definitely a minori
she was assigned to mopping, waxing and buffing the floo
cleaning the toilets, basically working as a maid. She was one
three black waves on the base, technically two, because one of th
girls was passing for white (it came out when her mother paid h
an unannounced visit and she was a black woman) and she di
not fraternize with the rest of the black girls.

Mia was there during the height of discrimination in th
barracks, so she developed a strong, determined demeanor, so sh
would not be taken advantage of and it came off as the big bul
type.

For example things were so bad that she gave her a Captains ast for applying and getting the job as a Dental Hygienist in the ental Department. Mia saw an ad for the job of Dental Hygienist the base newspaper and took the liberty to call and schedule an erview appointment. She went during her lunch hour and was ven the job. When the Dental Clinic recruiter called the Barracks hief to confirm her employment and get a start date for her, the rracks Chief went ballistic.

She stalked up to Mia grabbed her shoulder and said who ve you permission to go and apply for that job? That is subordination; you are getting a Captains Mast. Mia had the ptains Mast and received three weeks restriction, which meant e could only go to work and to the mess hall no where else base. She had to bring all her civilian clothes to the Chief she could lock them up in her office. Now it was the Chief's sponsibility to place the girls on jobs on the base as they opened . But she only placed the white girls all the black girls worked housekeepers in the barracks in the morning then they would over to the Mess Hall to peel potatoes in the afternoon.

So after her restriction Mia went into on the job training and orked as a Dental Technician in the Dental Department which as upstairs over the Medical Department were Buck worked at's how they met and fell in love. They made great plans, she was ing to get a good civilian job and support Buck while he went to edical school. After he became a doctor they were going to have e white house with the picket fence and 2 children they had a eam but it turned into a nightmare after a few years of marriage. ior to falling for Buck, Mia had been madly, head over heels in ve with a big tall dark and handsome marine named Ricky. Mia ought he was her soul mate. She said he could do things to her e had never experienced before in her life, he made her weak in e knees. But as much as she cared for him she also had a fear of m because he had a violent streak that became evident whenever drank too much. After he knocked Mia up, she asked him what ey were going to do about it. He told her they were going to go vay one weekend and get married as soon as he could get leave, he ld her don't worry about it, but he was only stalling for time.

After she was two months along and he still hadn't made a
effort to save her good name, she asked one of the waves on ba
that worked in the personnel office to check his personnel recor
and find out about his background. The wave came back and to
Mia that Ricky was married and had several children it seeme
by all the allotments coming out of his paycheck. Mia was crush
she felt like she was dying. She really cared for this man, wh
was she to do? She called her mother and told her the situati
she was in and was told to come home immediately. So M
put in a request to take leave and went home. Her mother ha
made arrangements to terminate the pregnancy on her end. A
soon as Mia stepped off the plane her mother whisked her off
keep the appointment. Upon arrival at the doctor's office whe
the procedure was to take place as soon as the doctor saw her I
started shaking his head no, he refused because there was M
standing there in her military uniform, so they had to go back
the house and make other arrangements and Mia changed cloth
They arrived at the next scheduled appointment in civilian cloth
and they were able to get the job done quick, fast and in a hur
After two weeks of rest and relaxation Mia flew back to the ba
to resume her military life.

As soon as Ricky heard Mia was back on base and lookin
good, he got busy calling her and stalking her coming to the wa
barracks unannounced requesting she be paged. When she wou
appear he would start pressuring her for dates and sex, so she we
to see the base Chaplin and told him that Ricky was harassing h
and she was scared of him.

The Chaplin checked Ricky's records and noticed he was
married man with a family and he had him shipped off to anoth
base far away in the desert within the same week.

Several months later Mia met Buck and they started to da
and got serious. Mia got pregnant and didn't want to go throug
that procedure again so she and Buck got married at the ba
Chapel by the Chaplin she had confided in. She had a ni
wedding it was well put together even though she had no he
from her immediate family.

Mia moved with her new husband Buck off base to Berkeley. ıt she still had to work on base and to stand duty on some ekends. When Mia had to stand duty on base she would stay the transient barracks so that was how she and Cheri became ch good friends (remember Cheri spent quite some time in the ınsient barracks).

Mia would come into the room and take off her clothes then ıke Cheri up, telling her she was going to be late for work. Cheri ing sleep deprived from cavorting every night at the Club until closed, would jump up and run down the hall to the head, take shower and brush her teeth come back take the rollers out of r hair and get fully made up and dressed only to find out it was)0pm not am. Cheri was exhausted from getting up early in the orning to go to work. Some times she would try to catch a ten inute nap at lunch in the ladies room on the couch if somebody se didn't beat her to it. Cheri was so tired that when she went her room after work to lie down and take a nap, she would fall to such a deep sleep that Mia or Fanny would pull that same .ck on her all the time; waking her up and telling her she was ing to be late for work or inspection, and Cheri being so tired ouldn't know if it was evening or early morning. She would just mp up running helter skelter.

Once the novelty wore off, Cheri would just rise up from h
bed and tell them to close her doors and leave her alone, after
how long can you do the same joke? Since Mia had an apartme
and no friends in town she turned to the waves on the base f
company. When Mia and Buck furnished their apartment th
only bought pieces of furniture that converted into beds. They h
a chair and ottoman that converted into a single bed, a couch th
converted into a double bed, so they were able to have multip
people sleeping over at any given time. Their only guests we
always waves from the barracks. Cheri would take the bus fro
the front gate of the base into downtown Oakland and Mia wou
pick her up at the bus terminal. After Mia got her drivers licen
she would drive to the base and pick up Cheri for the weekenc
On those weekends they would cook all kinds of foods, see Che
could cook and Mia and Fanny could not, so they would literal
argue over whose apartment she would be coming to for t
weekend.

One Fourth of July they wanted to Bar B Que and since th
did not have a grill nor could they afford one, they dug a hole
the ground in the backyard of the apartment building and fill
it with charcoal they took the rack out of the oven and placed
over the hole and cooked three slabs of ribs. They were so hung
for some home cooking that they had purchased a slab of ribs f
each one of them and they ate ribs until they got tired and th
were delicious. The next day on base Cheri was feeling crazy an
she kept experiencing strange sensation around her heart, so sh
had to go to the Medical Department for heart flutters, after sh
told the doctor what she had eaten the doctor said her proble
came from consuming all that pork.

Another time they cooked a pot of chitterlings and made leslaw, candied yams and a pan of jiffy cornbread, Mia's silly ısband "Buck" made the mistake of telling one of the guys on e base what they were cooking and how he couldn't wait to get me to eat. Well the guy he told what was waiting for him at me, told everybody he came in contact with, so as soon as the ls had finished cooking the meal and were about to set the ole so they could sit down and eat when Buck got there, there s a loud knock at the door. Mia and Cheri exchanged a look d said at the same time that can that be? They knew it wasn't ıck because he had a key to his own front door.

Upon peeking out the kitchen window (their apartment was the first floor) they saw what appeared to be at least twenty ys from the base standing at the door. Quick! Mia said gesturing th her hands at Cheri to put up the food.

Mia went to answer the door stalling for time by asking them ıat they were doing at her house. She said what's going on and ıy were they here she wasn't having a party. As she blocked their w with her body, Cheri meanwhile was busy hurrying about in e kitchen putting the food away and in her haste she put the ld stuff in the oven and the hot stuff in the refrigerator. Mia ıally let them in after exchanging silly banter for a few minutes. ıey all sat down, some of them sat on the floor some on the cktail table, some on the arms of the couch and chairs, while ey continued to made idle chatter. The girls pretended they dn't cooked anything as if those guys couldn't smell the food, pecially the pungent odor of chitterlings.

Mia and Cheri had to sit there and entertain those hungry oking men with light chatter for at least two hours before Buck ıally came home. They managed to out sit those guys and after e few remaining guest left they were finally able to eat the meal, t the long wait had spoiled it for them. It didn't taste the same, hen you have a taste for something and you have to wait too ng to get it, it looses the flavor.

Because Cheri had the job at the base theatre she had mo
money to spend than most of the other girls. She made mo
money from the theatre than she was getting from Uncle Sa
this enabled her to go into town to shop at the upscale stores.
when she felt like it Cheri would call her friend Mia and ask
her to meet her bus at the bus station downtown so they cou
go shopping. One Saturday afternoon after having worked
morning at the theatre stacking the new orders of candy a
supplies, Cheri came back to the barracks went into her room a
disrobed, she put on her robe and slippers and her shower cap a
grabbed a towel and her soap and was about to leave her roo
heading for the shower when Dora suddenly appeared in t
doorway. She stood there grinning at Cheri with her gold too
smile, looking sly and sneaky her pop eyes shifting all around t
room as she asked Cheri what's going on. Cheri told her nothi
was going on, she was about to take a shower and catch the b
into town. Dora said oh! OK, well I'll see you later as she slu
away down the hall. So Cheri continued on to the shower. Ch
had stopped hanging around with Dora many months previou
she didn't care for her as a person anymore. Cheri took a go
long hot shower because she felt tired and her shoulders ach
from lifting those heavy boxes of candy and popcorn oil.

After her shower she returned to her room she got dressed took r purse out of the locker where she had left it, closed the locker ors and left her room to catch the base bus into town. Upon her ival at the bus terminal, she got off the bus and climbed into r friend Mia's Thunderbird car and off they went to spend the ernoon shopping and sharing girl talk. After browsing through e stores Cheri finally saw something she liked and decided to ake a purchase, when Cheri went to pay for her purchase she covered she had no money! Not a dollar bill! All Cheri had s some loose change in her wallet; she had been robbed by the rracks thief........Dora. Cheri wanted to have Dora killed she s so mad. Cheri was sick and tired of that black, skinny, ugly oman trying to play her for a fool. First she was stealing her othes out of her room and wearing them whenever she wanted without her permission. Then when Cheri would confront her out it, she would smile in her face saying I'll get them cleaned n't worry. Now taking all her money this was the last straw.

That ugly demon had left her with nothing but her Navy check ich she hadn't cashed because she hadn't had time to go to the nk. Since Cheri made more money at the theatre than she t from the Navy she had been saving it up to go shopping for eeks, so Dora had got her real good for at least several hundred llars. Cheri told Mia what had happened and they both vowed get that evil black bitch. They didn't understand how a person uld be so treacherous to someone who has been nothing but ce to you. Cheri had let Dora borrow outfits of hers sometimes ien she had something special to go to, she had befriended that onster and this was her reward, robbed and stabbed in the back! heri vowed to never trust anybody again since they all have terior motives.

Mia had her baby while Cheri was at home on two weeks lea
during the summer it was a stroke of luck that Cheri had decid
to come back to the base a few days early to rest before going ba
to work. When she arrived at the barracks, she learned that M
had had the baby from one of the other waves that had come
contact with Buck on the base. Cheri went to the payphone a
called and talked to Mia, she told her she had just got back to t
base, but as soon as she showered and changed her clothes, s
was on her way over to her apartment. When Cheri got to t
apartment Mia answered the door in tears, she didn't know t
first thing about what to do with a baby. Mia was an only chi
she had no knowledge of how to take care of a baby. Cheri ca
in like gangbuster and she completely took over, bathing the ba
and helped Mia prepare the bottles, making the formulas.

Mia said it was like a gift from heaven to open the door and s
Cheri standing there, she was so moved she asked Cheri then a
there to be the baby's godmother. Cheri and Mia's relationsh
had become extremely close they were more like sisters than ju
good friends who started out as enemies. Cheri was the sist
that Mia never had. Mia's husband also referred to Cheri as h
little sister he liked the fact that she could cook and was teachi
Mia how to cook different things. When Cheri came over Bu
knew he would be getting a decent meal that night something
didn't get often. That's why he didn't mind Cheri always hangi
around on weekends in fact he would pick her up himself if M
couldn't do it.

Buck was always trying to pair Cheri up with one of t
young Interns from the Medical Center where he worked sin
his discharge from the Navy as an X-Ray Technician, the trade
had learned in the Navy. When Cheri found out that the inter
only made a small amount of money she was not interested at a
She was looking for a man with money. Boy was she stupid, tho
guys would be eligible to make a fortune later on down the ro
but at the present time she wasn't into forecasting the future
was all about her and right now.

CHAPTER 9

Fanny

ANNY WAS CHERI'S OTHER BEST buddy; they were both ly and wild as hell. They got a kick out of smoking cigarettes d talking about men. Fanny was dating Bart (the guy that was oking at the Club) he was much older than Fanny and she was azy about him. Sine she was only Twenty years old the girls ought that maybe she was looking for a father figure.

Fanny was a pretty girl; she had almond shaped eye and a aches and cream complexion and was average height. She wore r naturally curly hair cut short and even though she was skinny e had a big derriere and she was very naïve. She was the ultimate mme fatale, rolling her eyes and laughing up at the guys. Fanny d been a cheer leader in high school before joining the Navy d she took great pride in that accomplishment. She loved to ut around in high heel shoes at all times. Fanny was the type girl she was lost without a man in her life, if she broke up th her boyfriend this afternoon, she would be dating someone se tonight she had no trouble getting men. Cheri found Fanny using by her determination to always have a man.

Fanny also worked for the Military Police Station along wi Tammy. Fanny and Cheri use to go down to the barracks kitch and ramble through the community refrigerator to see what th could find to eat when they were hungry and didn't want to g dressed in their uniforms to go to the Mess Hall. One Saturd morning they found some breakfast sausage and eggs so th decided to cook and eat them. While in the process of takii the last few bite of the food a wave came in and started lookii through the refrigerator for her food only to find it missing. T girl was standing in front of the fridge fussing about her missii food, when Fanny shifted her almond shaped eyes at Cheri ai said that's a damn shame, a person can't put anything in th refrigerator and come back and get it.

Cheri was almost choking on her food trying to keep fro laughing because she knew that they were the ones who h cooked it and was about finish eating it. Fanny was famous f getting the older guys to get her beer at the Club, since she w underage. And she was forever getting chased out of the bus st huts for making out with her boyfriends but she was a lot of fu and they were young. After Fanny and Bart broke up, she start going to the Club and dancing with the rest of them, that's hc she happen to meet Dan.

Dan was tall, dark and handsome and he had a lot of rank. F was next in line to go up for the rank of Chief and he drove a ne convertible car. Dan was a liar and a fool and he was fascinat with Fanny, he liked the way she looked, she was light skinn and had pretty hair and a big butt, plus she seemed like she w hot to trot. Dan seemed so much more mature than the guys th were use to fooling around with and he was. He was more matu because he was so much older then they were he had lied abo his age. He told them he was twenty-five when he was almc forty.

If the girls hadn't been so silly and had been paying attention details other then dancing and acting wild and crazy they would ve figured it out by the hash marks on his sleeves. You get one sh mark for every four years of service; the man had four which eant he had already served sixteen years of military service while ey only had a year or two under their belt. There was no way ssible he could have been twenty-five years old with sixteen ars of service, did he enlist at the age of nine?

Fanny and Dan spend most of their dates at the different hotels d motels up and down the coast line since Dan was stationed so away. So after weeks of pining for each others company and ggling off time to be together they eloped to Reno.

Since Dan had a new convertible car with four in the floor and taught Fanny how to drive a stick shift. Fanny would entice heri to ride with her up the California coast eighty miles one ty so she could see her new husband by telling her that they had better selection of guys at Moffitt Field and their dances were ore lively and fun than what would be going on at Treasure land. It wasn't true, Fanny just didn't like taking that long drive herself, so they would go together and after the dance was over d Dan was off duty, he and Fanny would drive all the way back the coast to drop Cheri off at Treasure Island. So all total they re driving two hundred and forty something miles round trip st to be together.

Shortly after the marriage, Dan on one of his many trips to e wave barracks at Treasure Island to pick up his wife, (Fanny is still staying in the wave barracks on base because they had not und an apartment yet) saw Cheri in the lounge and told her he inted her to meet one of his friends. He said he had one named oah who would be perfect for her and he was wealthy. He said had owned his own filling station before he got called in for tive duty, he was in the reserves. Dan also said that Noah was llege educated and was suppose to take a job in Hawaii when he t called in for active duty and he had two foreign cars. Cheri's ght eyebrow went up she was impressed; she said yes I'd like to eet him.

Eventually Dan found an apartment for Fanny and hims
in a nice area of Berkeley. He was able to afford a really ni
apartment since he made a lot more money than most of the gu
in the military. Most of them were only a Seaman (E-2) with
more than a years service while he was a Chief (E-6) with mo
than sixteen years of service and he was old real old.

After Dan and Fanny got settled into their apartment D
would drive Fanny to Treasure Island on Monday for work, th
travel on to Moffitt Field where he stayed on base until he ca
back home on Friday evenings, unless he had the watch and cou
not leave the base. Since he was gone most of the time Dan lik
for Fanny's friends to come over and keep her company.

Fanny got pregnant immediately after getting married a
applied for discharge in her second trimester it was granted
she was in her apartment from Monday thru Friday eveni
alone. She would call up to the base and ask Cheri to come ov
every weekend because she didn't know anybody in the apartme
building. Sometimes Cheri would go over on Friday and stay un
Sunday evening when Fanny and Dan would drive her back
Treasure Island. Other times Cheri would spend the weekend
Mia's apartment. Those girls were playing tug of war with Ch
for her company and her culinary skills they would start calli
on Thursday to see who could get to her first and get mad wh
she went someplace else other that to their houses. When Ch
would go over to Fanny's they would go shopping or cook t
different foods that Fanny was craving while she was waiting
give birth. Dan also liked the fact that the girls came over, becau
this enabled him to be free to run around with his friends wh
he was home for the weekend he could drink and take acid.

Fanny was so young and naïve she believed anything Dan told
r. She thought he was the messiah or something because he
›uld just think of a lie and tell it to her and she believed it. Once
wanted to buy some more beer and she told him he had had
ough for one day and asked him not to buy anymore. He said
:. I am going to go to the store with my friend Moe, she said
e just don't buy any more beer today. An hour later Dan walked
to the apartment and said in a loud excited voice look what I
und laying on the side of the road; it was a six pack of frosty
: cold beer, with one can missing from the pack. She must have
lieved him because she started laughing, saying that he sure
ıs lucky to find beer when he wanted some more so bad, it was
parent he was lying about the beers and he looked at Cheri and
.nked his eye.

Fanny thought she had hit the jackpot; she had an older mature
an who made pretty good money taking care of her and he loved
clean the apartment. Dan was over the laundry department on
e ship he was stationed on; so he took their dirty linens to work
.d laundered them aboard ship, which meant Fanny did not
.ve to clean the apartment or do the laundry. Dan would scrub
e kitchen for hours on end. It was a Pullman Kitchen very small
st big enough to cook in, little did she know that he was high on
ugs, (drug users have no sense of time) which accounted for his
ing in the kitchen for hours on end. After all how long does it
ke to clean the stove and wipe off the refrigerator and wipe up
five by eight kitchen floor Fanny was never the wiser or at least
e didn't act like she knew. Cheri found out because Dan asked
:r to take some pills with him once when he was mopping and
-mopping the kitchen floor, he said he didn't want to take the
.p by himself.

Cheri had declined his offer in a nice way, she didn't want offend him since he was a good friend to her and was one of h best friend's husbands. But Cheri had an aversion to people wh couldn't control themselves and she felt that people who us drugs or alcohol had no self control plus they must be down rig stupid to ingest that poison into their bodies. Fanny's apartme came furnished, so they didn't have to buy furniture. It was spacious one bedroom apartment with a bed that came down o of the wall behind double doors in the living room, which made look like the space was a double size closet but when you opene the doors and pulled the bed down you had a full size bed. Th bed is where Cheri slept when she stayed over to their house. T only problem with the situation was that it was in the living roo so if she got sleepy she would had to wait until everybody el went to bed before she could pull the bed down out of the wa and go to sleep, luckily they didn't have much company comi over besides herself. Fanny loved to watch television especial murder mystery movies, she would watch them all day and a evening up into the wee hours of the morning before she becan tired and would go to bed. Then Fanny said she couldn't get u before twelve o'clock noon, if she did she would get a headach Cheri was use to getting up early in the morning and would ha to amuse herself until Fanny got up when she went over to h apartment.

At first Dan didn't mind Fanny wallowing in bed half the da he wanted her in the bed; he did not want his new wife out of th bed until after the bloom wore off the rose; then he became dow right cruel to her. Dan would make nasty remarks to Fanny abo her being out of shape and he would call her an animal.

While Fanny was pregnant she had severe morning sickness, d sometimes she couldn't make it to the bathroom. Once she rew up in the kitchen sink and he ranted and raved about it weekend talking about how nasty that was. Cheri felt they ere ill suited for each other but she didn't get involved, it was eir choice to marry they picked each other, although it made r uncomfortable when he would say nasty things to his wife in r presence. Fanny was young and inexperienced and Dan was der and mature and had been around the block more than once. heri thought to herself that those girls shouldn't have gotten arried so soon. First of all they didn't know the first thing about ing married. There was more to being married than just being le to have sex whenever you felt like it, those girls couldn't even ok they didn't know the first thing about sharing an abode with man. They were not familiar with making small talk with a sband or sharing ideas for the future or how to balancing a dget, or about paying bills all they knew was that they were free have sex, so these unions were doomed to fail. They were just ilures looking for a place to happen and having a child to add to e equation was not a smart move.

Since Fanny had no family around she turned to Cheri for oral support and someone to bounce questions off of when she d one. But then what did Cheri know? She had practically experience with men, the only thing she was familiar with as dressing and dancing and talking crazy, anything on an timate level was Greek to her. Cheri didn't know beans about lationships she had never had a real relationship and didn't want ne. The only thing she was interested in was enjoying life and opping, she went shopping every week to get new outfits to ear to the base dances.

One Saturday evening Dan picked up Fanny and Cheri an
took them back to Moffitt Field; to the Enlisted Men's Club f
one of the local dances (all bases have an EM Club). When th
walked into the Club it was filled to with people. There was a I
on the stage spinning the latest records and some people we
dancing while others were just milling around talking. Cher
eyes scanned the dimly lit room looking for some place to s
when she noticed an empty table and some chairs off to the sic
and in one of the chairs slouched down with a boring as hell lo
on his face was one of the handsomest brown skinned guys Che
had seen in a long, long, time.

He was a high tan color with a keen features and his light ey
were to die for, plus he was tall about 6'6" slim built and wearin
a suit. A real civilian suit; he looked like a handsome wealth
playboy totally out of place in that Club. Cheri couldn't he
thinking damn he is fine and he looks like he has money, nc
this is somebody you could take home to Momma. Dan start
grinning as he walked over to the man and said, "Hey Man" wha
going on? He didn't give him time to answer before he said let m
introduce you to my little sister (all the males referred to Cheri
their little sister), this is Cheri, Cheri meet my man Noah. Cher
heart was beating at least fifty miles a minute but she managed
keep her exterior cool and calm. Never let them think you we
interested in them never let them see you sweat. After all she ha
been programmed with the fact that waves don't show emotion
she had that down pat. Noah untangled his long frame from th
chair and stood up and his whole expression changed as he brok
into a smile while starring at them.

Cheri could see he had nice teeth and his light brown ey
twinkled when he turned to her and said pleased to meet yo
She smiled back at him and said likewise. Cheri was glad sh
had taken extra precaution with her attire and her hair that nigh
she knew she looked and smelled real good. Noah asked her
dance and they did to a slow number then they made small ta
for awhile before he asked for her phone number.

Cheri gave him the number to the payphone on the first ck (she only gave the first floor phone number to people she lly wanted to talk to, the second floor phone was for any and erybody) then he said still smiling at her the next time I come the Bay area I will give you a call. She was instantly miffed, but e didn't let it show, she just smiled back at him and said alright t she was thinking "**When he comes to the Bay area he will ve me a call**", he must be a damn fool! I am not on hold waiting this arrogant bastard he can kiss my ass.

While they had been dancing and talking Dan and the other lows had been making bets that Cheri couldn't do anything th Noah, because he was out of her league. He was active in neighborhood church, played the organ on Sundays in church ten he was available and he didn't curse. Everybody who knew heri knew she cursed like a sailor, every other word out of her outh was a curse word and she was quick to anger and did not go church. Noah was soft spoken, low key and appeared polished, d he didn't really mingle with the other military personnel on se. His family lived in Oakland that's where he was from, so he ould go home when he had free time. That's what he had meant ten he said when he comes to the Bay Area he would give her a ll, she just didn't know it.

A call from Moffitt Field to Treasure Island was a real, real, ng distant call. That phone call would be measured by each nute so a fifteen or twenty minute phone call could cost him e or more dollars which is a lot for a man who at the time was ly making forty dollars every two weeks.

Chapter 10

Travis Air Force Base

Cheri told some of the other waves at Treasure Islar
about a free bus that transported civilian women from the Oaklar
and San Francisco area to Travis Air Force Base for dances c
Friday evenings. She had found the flyer in the ladies room
one of the department stores when Mia and she had been in tov
shopping. The bus left from in front of the California Hotel
7:00pm on Friday evenings. The Friday they planned to go, Che
Tammy, Angela and a couple of other girls caught the base b
from Treasure Island to Oakland and made their way over
the California Hotel. Since they had gotten there early Tamn
suggested they walk down the street to a liquor store which th
did, Tammy went into the store and purchased two bottles
Silver Satin Wine and a package of kool-aid. She poured t
kool-aid into one of the bottles of wine and shook it up and th
all drank some of it, it tasted good like fruit pop.

The girls were able to board the bus to Travis with no proble
along with the rest of the civilian women because they we
wearing civilian clothes not their uniforms (they didn't wear the
when they went out). The people running this particular operati
had it geared for civilian not military women. It was basically
way to get females to the airmen stationed on the air base whi
was located seventy or so miles from Oakland.

Since most of the girls in the sixties didn't have transportation
vas the perfect way to get them to the base which they wouldn't
dinarily have been able to get to. The girls were feeling no pain
the bus ride to Travis Air Force Base, once they arrived at the
se and got off the bus they didn't see Cheri until it was time to
.ve. She had gotten diarrhea from drinking the wine and had
ent the entire time of the dance which lasted four hours in the
lies room every time she tried to leave the restroom she had to
back into it. They decided to go again the following Friday but
ıen they caught the bus Cheri was ready, she refused the wine.
hen they got to Travis and went into the Club where the dances
ıere held, they didn't get a chance to survey their surroundings
fore all these guys came rushing over asking them to dance. It
.s too many of them coming up all at once that made Cheri feel
ry; one man right after another kept asking her to dance.

Cheri could sense something wasn't right so she refused to
nce with them using the excuse that she was not ready to dance
t; to Cheri it felt like a setup. While standing around watching
e people do the latest dances and talking to some random guys
awhile, one young man walked over and gave her the once
er looking her up and down before he spoke and said you lose
ın; she didn't take the bait, she didn't dance. Cheri found out
er by talking to him one on one that they had made a bet with
oney about how long it would take them to get the girls to dance.
ıeri was offended not for herself, but for the fact that these girls
d ridden on that damn bus, traveled all this distance to dance
d interact with a bunch of damn fools. These fools didn't even
spect them as decent females who had come to socialize with
me supposedly lonely airmen.

Apparently there must have been a need for someone to through the process of renting buses and printing flyers to rou up young civilian women and bring them seventy or so miles o way just to interact with them and this is how they act! So this what they think of the civilian women just a bunch of silly gi to be made a fool of. Cheri was feeling salty but she continu to talk to this guy getting information, while standing off to t side of the dance floor and perusing the room for better prospec and there weren't any. She found out he was from New York, h name was Artis and when they turned up the lights she could s that he was so handsome it was ridicules. At first glance she h thought he was Italian until he spoke, he was very fair skinn and had a roman nose which fit his face perfectly, it seemed th all his features looked like they had been chiseled to perfection a sculptor, he was medium height no more than 5'8", very slig built almost petite in size and he had really nice jet black sil hair with a slight curl on the ends. They talked and danced t three hours away and became quite infatuated with each other, commented on the fact that since they were both slight built th would fit perfectly together. She found herself laughing at h corny jokes, and giggling when he would make fun of the oth guys saying things like he had the prettiest girl there and ho lucky he had gotten that evening, to Cheri flattery will get yo everywhere. When it was time to re-board the bus back to Sa Francisco Cheri felt a little let down she was beginning to enjoy being with Artis. So they exchanged telephone numbers an shared one sweet exquisite kiss before parting; with him sayin I will definitely be calling you. Cheri never saw him physical again after that night, but they talked on the phone for three an four hours every night for at least a month.

The girls that lived on the second floor along with Cheri were rious at her for always tying up the phone at night. After she me in from work at the Theatre, she would shower and change to her pajamas and wait around for her evening phone call from tis that came on time every night; and when she got on the one the rest of them couldn't use it until after midnight when e would hang up and go to bed. Artis had a friend that worked e main switchboard at Travis and he would hook him up to her mber in San Francisco because that was a real long distance call d in California they charged by the minute and there was no y he could have afforded two and three hour phone call. After nding in that small tight phone booth with no seat, holding the ceiver so long to her ear Cheri's arm would be aching the next y at work.

Artis was stationed at Travis Air Force Base but he was assigned the hospital, the military was in the process of discharging m from the Air Force with a medical discharge because he had epatitis B. Looking back Cheri realized how young and dumb e had been, to be oblivious to his health problems and having idea nor caring to find out what exactly hepatitis was. Thank d she had only kissed him once that shit is deadly. After talking th him for a little over a month one weekend Cheri went to town to spend the weekend with her friend Mia, when she turned she found out that he had been calling all that weekend st about every hour from Friday evening to Sunday afternoon. tis had gotten discharged and had traveled to San Francisco nting to see her. He went to an uncle's house in San Francisco d when he couldn't reach her after trying for two days, he had ught a flight home to New York City.

He left probably thinking she had just been bullshitting hi over the phone and that she was just another party type g who went out with different guys on the weekends and did come back until Monday when it was time for her to go ba to work. Anyway they never did get to reconnect and she nev heard from him again. Cheri had some trepidation about how t whole scenario had gone down that weekend. Since Angela t snake had been handling Cheri's calls all weekend there was telling what she had said to him. It just seemed kind of fishy sin she knew exactly where Cheri was staying and had the numb Cheri had been at Mia's house which was only across the brid from San Francisco. Cheri pondered as to why she hadn't call her to tell her Artis was looking for her or give Mia's number Artis? Angela knew how Cheri felt about Artis because they h discussed the situation. Anyway Cheri called the number he h left for his uncle's house and was told by the uncle that Artis h left to go home after he couldn't reach her.

Cheri was more than a little disturbed since they had be so close and yet so far away. Angela had no life and was alwa in the barracks when she didn't have a date which wasn't th often and she was jealous of Cheri more than Cheri knew. Ch never got to talk to Artis again and she never forgot him but s had to move on, after all they were not that deeply involved th had only been in each others presence once, and she was in t military surrounded by guys. New guys came and went from t base every day so it didn't take much to be forgotten just bei absent from sight would do it Cheri never went back to Travis A Force Base again.

CHAPTER 11

Noah

NE SUNDAY EVENING CHERI HAD just come in from working
r shift at the base theatre when it was announced over the PA
stem that she had a phone call first deck. Her antennas' went
she knew instantly who it was because she hardly ever got
ls on the first deck. She lived upstairs so she used the second
ck phone for local calls. The girls having heard the page and
owing the phone setup all came running to her room they were
cited (some were envious) for her.

Cheri's slipper clad feet hardly touched the steps as she rushed
wn the two flights of stairs to answer the phone, she was in
ch a hurry that she hit her hip on the thick wooden banister, it
de such a loud cracking noise that she thought she had broken
r hip, the instant pain was breath taking and searing but she
ged on to the first floor phone booth. Even though she was out
breathe from running and in excruciating pain from cracking
r hip bone she picked up the receiver and said very calmly and
eetly "Hello". It was Noah calling, he said he had come home
the weekend and hoped he would be able to see her before he
d to head back up the coast to Moffitt Field. Cheri was so out
breathe that periodically she would place the receiver to her
driff while she took deep breaths between sentences, before
ntinuing their conversation.

They made a date that very minute and he said he would
over to the base within thirty minutes to pick her up; they sa
their goodbyes and hung up the phone. Cheri had to hurry! S
smelled like butter popcorn, her hair needed curling and her h
was hurting like crazy, but since she had to shower and get dresse
she had one girl pressing her clothes, another helping her get h
hair together and another helping to apply her makeup. Wh
it was announced over the PA system that she had a guest in t
lounge thirty minutes later; she looked fabulous as she stroll
across the quarterdeck to the lounge to greet her date and out t
door they went and climbed into his waiting car. She looked li
it had taken no effort at all to be that pulled together in so short
period of time, like she was always together and was able to pi
up and go at a moments notice.

Noah drove them up to a place called lookout point at Berkeley
iiversity and they sat in the car on the hill looking out at the
yline view of the city talking and listening to the music on the
dio for hours. Noah told her he liked her style and that he was
to writing music and planned to return to school when his tour
duty was up. But when he tried to sing a song he was writing
her, he had to chuckle at the fact that he couldn't seemed to
member the words to his own song and he said it was because
her. She smiled coyly up at him because she got a kick out
the fact that she could have that kind of impact on a man.
fter he told her about the song, Noah slipped his arm around
r shoulders and gently pulled her in close for a kiss, he had been
inking about it since he picked her up at the barracks. He had
is overwhelming desire to taste her lips. The kiss turned into
veral kisses, and they were both breathless when he released her
d he said since had he met her she had gotten into his head
bad that he couldn't even remember what he was writing or
inking, and that she was all he had been thinking about these
st few weeks. Cheri smiled feeling safe and warm snuggled in
oah's arms she felt an attraction to him too, even though she
dn't thought about him since she had met him. If he hadn't
lled tonight he would have still been forgotten. But now being
close in each others faces she felt differently about him and she
uld smell the slight hint of garlic on his breath and for some
ason she didn't find it repulsive even though Cheri detested the
iell of garlic.

Cheri liked Noah because he was handsome and dressed we
He seemed nice and ambitious and he was a gentleman or
she thought. Noah liked Cheri because she was always nice
dressed and pulled together and she acted so ladylike, so demu
and she smelled damn good too. He felt that not only was s
very attractive but that she had a lot of class. Cheri talked abo
her home life like she came from somewhere, it was apparent th
everybody came from somewhere, but she made it sound like s
came from money, old money. Cheri knew how to handle herse
well like she was only use to the best that life had to offer becau
that was what she was after the best. She was able to shop ar
could afford to have charge accounts at the high end stores li
The Whitehouse, Mademoiselle, Bennioff's, I. Magnum and s
only wore shoes by Andrew Gellar because she had two jobs.

Cheri and Noah started dating regularly, they went to t
theatre a lot and to local dances, but he would never take her
meet his family. She thought about it periodically but she did
dwell on it, it didn't really matter that much to her because s
wasn't into that whole family thing anyway.

Cheri had spoken to his mother several times on the pho
and she had seemed pleasant enough but they had never met
person although his mom had expressed a desire to meet her. No
didn't want to get in to deep to soon. To him bringing a girl hon
meant something, something he wasn't ready for at this stage
the game he had plans for his life, he wasn't ready to commit. H
would take her to his parent's house when they weren't home
try and have sex with her of which she always refused. Che
would be thinking to herself; if I am not good enough to me
your family then you can fuck yourself.

Noah quit Cheri! After hanging out with her for sever
months, he was sick of not getting any loving all this girl want
to do was dance, laugh and talk in that exact order. Hell! He was
man he had needs. He was sick of walking around with the bl
balls.

One balmy Saturday evening he had picked her up from e wave barracks and taken her out to eat at a nice restaurant mething they didn't get to do often because of his finances, Cheri ıs feeling especially pretty that warm summer evening because e had just gotten her hair done earlier that morning and she ıs wearing one of her new designer outfits, while sitting there th her handsome boyfriend chatting and driving up the pacific ast highway. The warm light breeze blowing thru the open car ndows felt so good on her face that she leaned her head back ainst the seat cushion feeling safe and content. The soft pleated 'sey skirt of her suit fluttered lightly in the breeze caressing her ossed stocking encased legs, she felt special and relaxed on the ive back to the base. But Noah had a plan formulating in his ad, it had been swirling around in his brain all through dinner, ting across from her watching her eat and talk, batting her eyes him. So when he saw the sign flashing up ahead saying rooms ailable, he made his move. He pulled up at a motel entrance d put the car in park and turning to her he reached out and 'oked her left check lightly with the back of his hand as he ıiled and said should I get us a room? She looked him square his eyes and said No! Quite emphatically, so he got angry and id I can't see you anymore.

She sat up straight in the seat and said Oh! Your emotions ve a spigot on them that you can turn them off and on at will? 'ell if that's the way you feel you can just take me back to the rracks right now! They drove back in total silence, the mood d grown solemn and there was a chill in the air between them d when they reached the barracks she said goodbye and got out his car and slammed the door as hard as she could because she ıs trying to tear it off of his raggedy ass car. As she walked up e stairs and into the barracks she was feeling like shit inside but e would not give in to his demands.

Cheri was fucked up for weeks because she really, really lik
Noah. One Sunday afternoon several weeks later while Ch
was lazing around the barracks in her room, flipping throu
magazines or just starring into the mirror over her dresser
herself fiddling with her hair, she got a page for a phone call fi
deck. It was Noah, calling to ask her if she had called him. S
said "no" she hadn't called him. He said his mother told him so
girl had called while he had gone out to the store and he thoug
it was her. She said no it wasn't me, you told me you needed to
alone to clear your head and get your priorities in order, so w
would I call you? One thing I can do very well is not bother wi
people who do not want to be bothered with me.

Noah said he was at home because his mother was having
birthday dinner for him that day. He asked how she was doi
she said fine and they hung up the phone. Cheri went back up
her room feeling forlorn and deeply sad she felt like she want
to cry but about what? He wasn't worth her tears.

After she thought about it for a while she got mad becau
she was just getting over the man and he has the nerve to tur
around and call her up stirring up old feelings. That bastard w
having a birthday dinner and she was not invited. What a fucki
low life he was he just had to let her know he was having a party,
she's not invited why tell her about it at all. She vowed to hers
to fix his ass one way or another he would get his.

Noah called back the next week and they made a date to me
and talk and kind of clear the air between them. They both p
their feelings on the table on that date, he told her about thin
that she had had no knowledge of. Well one word led to anoth
and they decided to give the relationship another try since th
both genuinely cared about each other. It got better for a whi
Noah tried to make more time for Cheri, he really tried, but s
wanted more from him than he could possibly give at that tim
They didn't get to see each other often because of the distan
between them and Noah would take other peoples duty for ext
money.

Cheri was often left feeling frustrated and angry because
stead of spending time with her he was standing in for someone
e to make money. On Valentines Day he drove the eighty miles
er to her base just to bring her a box of candy and a kiss. He
uldn't stay long because he was standing someone else's duty
at night. He had driven over a hundred and sixty miles just to
ow her he really cared on Valentines Day.

Cheri was getting sick and tired of this shit real fast, she had
boyfriend but it was like she didn't have a boyfriend. The tale
the foreign car was a myth the car was so old it looked like a
eign car. And the man had no money he was always taking
ner peoples duty to make money to take her out

Meanwhile the bet was still on amongst the guys, they were
atching and waiting for Cheri to show out on Noah. It hadn't
ppened yet but it was bound to happen and they were still
iting and laughing behind his back and Dan was the main
stigator. Thanksgiving was approaching and Fanny and Cheri
ere planning to cook Thanksgiving dinner together for Dan
d Noah, at Fanny's apartment. They had gotten together one
ekend and planned their menu, purchased the food and split
e cost. Cheri had checked with Noah before she made any
ans to see if he would be free for the evening and had nothing
e pending other than to come to dinner at Fanny and Dan's
use. He said yes he was available and it sounded like it would
a fun evening.

Now Fanny is happy as a pig in slop, she is walking on air
cause she can't cook, and this will enable her to put on a nice
read for her new husband with all the fancy cooking being
ne by Cheri. On Thanksgiving eve, Noah came over to Fanny's
artment where Cheri was spending the weekend to take her to
e theatre. Cheri was busy in the bathroom putting the finishing
uches on her hair and makeup when he arrived, so Noah had
en sitting in the living room talking to Fanny and Dan. Upon
r entrance into the room Cheri noticed that Dan was sitting
ere smiling smugly like a big fat Cheshire cat when he suddenly
d Cheri! Noah said he is not coming to dinner tomorrow he
standing duty.

Some guy on base is paying him fifty dollars for taking h
holiday duty. Cheri stood there for what seen an eternity feeli
the heat rise from the pit of her stomach and go straight up to h
brain, she saw nothing but red as she felt the pent up fury starti
to surge through her body.

She forgot about the bet and every damn thing else that w
associated with it. All she wanted to do was kill this fucking fo
sitting there grinning up at her; if she had had a gun she wou
have shot him in his stupid grinning face point blank. She walk
over to where Noah sat grinning and stood over him while s
shouted **WHAT!** I asked you in plenty enough time and to
you what the plan was up front and you agreed to it, you sa
"OK" I am free that day **"Now"! "Today"!** The night before t
"Holiday" you tell me you are going to stand somebody's du
Well you can just kiss my ass, I am sick of your fucking shit.
want you to go straight to hell and get a fucking transfer so you c
keep on going and stay the hell out of my face you motherfucki
stupid ass bastard. Noah's expression changed as his eyes got b
as saucers. He swallowed several times before he said in a ve
soft controlled voice what's the matter with you? I am appall
at your language and your behavior then he started apologizi
to Fanny and Dan, and told Cheri they would discuss it furth
in the car.

After exiting the apartment, with Noah holding her firmly
the arm as he escorted her to his beat up waiting car and openi
the noisy rusty passenger side door he deposited her safely insi
Noah then walked around and got in the driver seat before
could speak, he was basically speechless he didn't know what
say to this angry girl.

Noah stole a sideways glance over at her as he turned the k
and started up the car, thinking what's gotten into her? She is
mad and she looks so pretty when she is angry. But how that ki
of language can come out of that pretty pouting mouth was beyo
his comprehension. He had never seen this side of her personali
before, it was intriguing to say the least knowing that she had
much fire pent up inside her it was a sign of raw passion.

She usually came off as unemotional and non-caring. In
:t he had gotten such a charge out of seeing and hearing her
›wup with such passion even in anger that he actually felt a
ep stirring in his loins. Wow! To know that she was not some
ld nonchalant, polite, prissy girl was very inspiring to Noah.
: thought to himself that if she had that much fire in her to
ict in such a way about him not being with her for dinner, what
›uld she let loose and turn into when he finally got her in a
ated sexual encounter. Noah was driving and thinking at the
ne time what his next move would be because he had to get
r in a bed. Finally speaking he asked what were you thinking
king like that in front of those people Noah asked. I thought
u were a lady. Cheri said I don't give a damn what you think,
u are nothing but a selfish, bullshit artist and I am sick of your
mb cheap ass.

Noah tried to explain to Cheri that this was an offer he
uldn't refuse, couldn't she see that he was making five times the
ing rate. He was getting fifty dollars for a four hour shift which
rmally paid ten dollars. After all he was only an E-1, which
:ant he only made forty dollars every two weeks, Cheri thought
herself, here he goes crying about his fucking situation again
d why he was so broke being in this man's Navy.

That shit didn't fly with Cheri anymore she knew that in order
make more money, normal enlisted people studied to pass the
ts they had to take to go up for more rank to get more pay. But
t "Mr. Noah" the military was beneath him, he was only killing
ne while fulfilling his obligation. Noah was in the reserves he
d been called in for active duty.

He only had twelve more months to serve and then he wou be getting discharged and be free, so he was not at all interested making more rank or anything else that had to do with the Na The date that night was awful, Cheri couldn't have told anyone they had asked what the movie had been about; she was too ups to even pay attention her boyfriend had embarrassed her, leavi her without a date for her own dinner party on Thanksgiving. S made a silent vow to herself that she would never try to act ni to please a man; she would never hide her true self again. If th don't like her for who she is they could go fuck themselves.

After that Thanksgiving fiasco, Cheri would date Noah on when and if she felt like it, at her leisure. After finding out t skinny on him, that he didn't own a filling station that he h been working there pumping gas, he didn't own a foreign car had been repossessed. He had taken some courses at Berkeley b had not finished with a degree. She was basically finished wi him. She held open season on his ass, sometimes she would cur whenever she felt like it just for the hell of it. She felt he was fraud, and she would not answer the phone when she knew was him calling. In essence she turned the tables on him and s started dating other guys, big time.

Noah requested and got orders to go out to sea for eig months this would shorten his shore duty. Everybody that kne Noah and had listened to him bitch and moan knew that would do anything short of murder to get out of the regular Na so he could get on with his life's plan. Cheri told him "bye" s you when I see you and she kept getting up, getting on with h own life. Noah would write her, but she knew it was just becau he was feeling lonely so she let him suffer she was not spendi her evenings writing back to him, when she felt like it she wou write but not in a timely manner.

Fanny wrote and told Dan that Cheri was dating two guys
ı the base and that were so handsome that they looked like
awaiians. Dan was on the same ship along with Noah out to sea
d he made sure that he passed the news along to Noah about
ıat was going on. Noah was so furious; he wrote a scathing
ter to Cheri asking her what was her problem? What's going
ı? What's with all these rumors he was hearing about her and
her guys while he was out to sea? Cheri avoided answering his
ıestions directly by writing back saying the last time she had
ecked she was not engaged or married and that she was free
ıgle and willing to mingle. Who did he think he was to question
r, he had never even introduced her to his family and they were
in close proximity to each other, they lived in Oakland and she
ıs stationed in San Francisco directly across the Bridge?

Cheri harbored a lot of animosity towards Noah because deep
wn inside she felt he was just stringing her along until he could
better. He had no future plans of them being together as a
uple; he was basically full of shit. It was all about Noah and
ıat he wanted to do but he got it wrong because as far as Cheri
ıs concerned it was all about her.

Noah thought he had it all figured out in his tiny mind of how
wanted to live the rest of his pretentious life. Cheri knew that
e didn't fit the mold as the woman of his dreams because of the
ıgth of time they had spent together and they were no closer
an if they had just met a few weeks ago. She felt he still was
rboring secrets about his true feelings for her because action
oke louder than words. So she was going to enjoy her military
e and go out and do whatever she felt like doing and if he didn't
e it so what!

Chapter 12

Lars

Cheri met Lars while working at the base theatre. Sin
Cheri and Abba were running the place they had requested fro
the powers that be, that they needed more help, their hours we
so tight that they couldn't take time off. They had to be the
seven days a week because the theatre was open everyday. O
evening Lars walked through the door of the theatre wearing h
navy blues and said he had just been hired by the manager, and
was told to come and shadow Abba until he was fully trained an
able to help run the base theatre operation Cheri couldn't he
but be slightly impressed by him. First because he was so tall an
well proportioned for his height and second he had the blue
eyes and blondest hair she had ever seen and third his teeth we
extremely white and straight; to sum it all up Lars was somethi
to look at. Cheri told him that since Abba was not at work yet
could start by collecting the tickets at the door and when thin
calmed down after the movie started she would show him how
fill the drink machines and measure out the oil for the pop co
machine.

Every day Lars showed up early to learned something new out the theatre operation, but he was learning it all from Cheri cause Abba always had something else to do or someplace else be. During the down time when the patrons would be in their ats watching the movie and the concession stand was closed heri learned about him. She found out that he also worked with bba in the Medical Department as a Corpsman during the day d he had a car and lived off base in San Francisco, and that bba had told him to ask the manager for the job at the theatre. rs told her he was from Iowa and was of German descent, and loved having brown sugar on and off his hot cereal.

When Lars made that statement Cheri glanced up coyly him and fluttered her long eyelashes she said that's nice and pt on counting the money in the cash drawer. As she counted e money against the cash register receipts Cheri was thinking out what Lars had said and how he had said it; she knew he s flirting with her. As time went on Abba was hardly at the eatre it was always Lars and Cheri, they got so familiar and mfortable with each other that he could tell whenever she made hange to herself. If she had been to the beauty shop and gotten new hairdo he made it his business to compliment her on it and r attire daily. He was always taking notice of the little things ost guys would take for granted especially if their not interested the person. Cheri wondered why he paid so close attention every detail. After Lars had been working with Cheri for a uple of months he asked her out on a date, she said no she was sy that night; all the while thinking he just wants to try and periment with me to see if the myth is true about black women ing hot to trot.

Although she did find him very attractive she decided to **"lea that alone"**. One evening while standing behind the count pouring soft drinks and putting out the candy before opening t theatre doors Cheri was feeling terrible and she looked it. She w having her monthly cycle and her back was killing her and s had a headache. Since she didn't like to take patent medicine s was just trying to dealing with it. Lars noticed she was draggi and not her normal peppy, upbeat self and asked her what w wrong? She told him she didn't feel well. He said why don't y take off and go back to the barracks and lay down until 10:30p when it was time to tally the receipts.

She thanked him for his concern; but said as she moved slow toward the ice cream cooler to sit on top of it, that she really did feel like walking over to the barracks and then have to walk ba later. Lars said can you drive? Cheri looked at him and said y so he said you can take my car, just make sure you come back lat to help me close up and so I'll have a way to get home tonight, said with a laugh as he reached into his pants pocket and took o the ring of keys. As he removed the key for the car and hand it to her their hands touched and their eyes met and a bond w formed at that moment between them. Cheri was thinking she went outside and climbed into Lars's car and drove the thr blocks over to the wave barracks that he's not so bad; in fact he alright. She parked the car in the last slot on the end in the wa barracks parking lot so she would be able to get out when it w time to go back to the theatre, she didn't need to have an accide with his car because she could drive but she didn't have a licens

Cheri entered the barracks and went straight upstairs to her
om not stopping to speak or talk to anyone. After opening
r locker doors for the privacy she craved, she walked over to
e windows and pulled the shades down. After kicking off her
oes she stretched out across her bed and dozed off. She had
en dozing off and on for about an hour when she was jarred
vake by a loud female voice in the hallway calling out "**Who is**
riving Lars's Car"? Cheri just laid there on her bed chuckling
herself thinking to herself why did that bitch care, she knew
the voice which girl was asking the question, the girl worked
the medical department with Lars. First of all Lars was not
arried and second he didn't date white girls and this girl was
finitely white, so why did she care? Maybe she liked him or
inted him for herself.

Cheri found this situation amusing as she laid there plotting
w she would return to the car. She knew the girl and her friends
ould be looking out the windows at the front end of the building
see who would be coming out and getting into the car, so she
anned to go out the back door and walk around to the end of
e parking lot were she had parked the car when she left. Any
y by the time she planned to go back to the theatre it would
dark outside, so they will never know "**WHO IS DRIVING**
ARS'S CAR"?

Cheri took the route she had planned and got back to the
eatre in time to assist Lars in cleaning up and counting the
gister receipts for the evening, he thanked her for being prompt
ming back. She looked at him like he was crazy and said I
ould be thanking you for letting me use your car. Lars said I felt
could trust you and you didn't fail me. Some people you can't
ist they'll say one thing and do another all they want to know
that you are not looking when they do something wrong. Lars
id you could have taken my car and gone into town and stayed
ntil you felt ready to come back, and all I would have been able
do is sit outside on the steps of this theatre and wait until you
turned with my transportation.

After they closed the theatre Lars gave her a ride over to tl Bank's night depository so she could make the money drop ar then he drove her to the wave barracks. She thanked him ar said see you tomorrow, he flashed a wide smile at her and said yo betcha. Lars sat and watched her go into the barracks before l drove off into the night thinking to himself I am going to get th girl to go out with me come hell or high water.

Cheri and Lars worked closely together for a few more wee before he built up his courage enough to make his move.

After rolling down the aluminum front to the concessio stand Lars reentered the area behind the counter and grabbed h around the waist and gave her a big kiss. At first she was shock and recoiled at his touch, but then she relaxed and melted into hi returning the kiss since the attraction was mutual. It became tl norm for them to finish up their work and spend a few minut making out before going their separate ways. When Lars ask her to go into town with him on a real date a few weeks later s did, and when they got to the front gate to go off base they had stop the car at the gate, the marine standing guard saluted the off as they drove away, they looked at each other and burst o laughing, thinking what a silly goose he was, didn't he know th were enlisted personnel just as he was.

The next day word had spread around the base like wildfi that some black wave was dating a white Commissioned Offic Cheri was just as anxious to know who it was as the rest of the they were all abuzz about who is was, it took Cheri and Lars week to realize they were talking about them. He had bought car that was previously owned by a Navy Doctor and it still h the caduceus on the license plate (the caduceus specified that tl person was an Officer) so they were talking about them, they g a big kick out of that.

One Friday night Cheri asks Tammy to double date with her
d Lars and his black civilian roommate. They were out having
good time until they stopped to park at a local parking spot
just sit and talk. That's what they were doing when a white
liceman shined his light into their car window. Lars rolled
wn the window and leaned his white blond head out of it and
ked him what the problem was?

The officer looked shocked and horrified but all he said was it
sn't safe for them to be parking there because some people had
en molested and robbed lately; he kept referring to Lars as sir
cause he also thought he was dealing with a white Officer.

They left the area and went over to Lars's apartment and
hile cuddling and kissing on the sofa Cheri asked Larry if he
uld take her home to his mother because she sure as hell could
t take him home to hers. He didn't have an answer for her so
just shrugged his shoulder and continued to gaze at her with
ose beautiful blue eyes. Cheri knew she would have to break
off with him because he didn't have the strength and she was
rting to have strong feelings for him and she didn't want to get
r feelings hurt. Cheri found out from that little fling with Lars
at it does not matter what color a person is if they treat you nice
u don't see color. All people really want is to be treated well and
spected as a human being.

Cheri had gotten to that comfortable place in her relationship
th Lars were she cared for him because he was a good man
ho acted like he was totally into her and he cherished her and
e liked it, too much. She broke off the relationship anyway
fore she really got in too deep. In the passing weeks Lars quit
rking at the theatre he couldn't deal with being around her and
t being able to kiss and hug her and she missed him too. She
ieved over the short time they had spent together because he
d made her feel like she was the most special girl in the world.
heri always felt that if Lars got married someday, it would be to
lack woman, because that was all he liked. After his fling with
heri, he started dating a wave name Emmy she was real cute and
inny and real real black.

Chapter 13

Vance

Cheri's job in the Receiving Station was to oversee tl
typing pool and to pass out the many forms to be filled out l
hand in pencil to the men coming back from overseas. The typi
pool workers would later type them up and they became offic
records for the men's personnel file. She would bark out the orde
loudly telling them what to put where on the forms, while walki
up and down in front of the counter which stretched about eig
feet long. She was an expert at telling people what to do tha
why the Warrant Officer had given her authority over that area
the typing pool. She had a way of speaking with authority in h
voice and she looked people straight in their eyes. It was most
for intimidation but it made people take notice and pay attentio
As Cheri was standing at the counter barking out her orders
the forty or fifty men who had just come in for processing arou
the corner and through the doors of the Receiving Station can
a battalion of men dressed in light blue cotton outfits. These m
were assigned to the Brig and they were being brought into tl
building for some kind of Court Marshal, apparently they h
done something they had no business doing; their charges cou
range from being AWOL to RAPE and even MURDER. Tl
man that was marching them to the court marshal area was
Swaggering Marine. He made quite a sight as he walked

raight and had his pants pulled up so high under his arms it was most humorous. He was equipped with a gun and baton (rumor is it if one of his prisoners gets away he has to serve the time). heri stopped talking to her men for a second to observe this fine ıman specimen she had an eye for beauty and he was beautiful. e was paper sack brown with an extraordinarily handsome ofile.

Under the hard visor hat he was wearing you could see he d heavy eyebrows that almost met in the center of his forehead d he had a keen nose and a small smug mouth with an ultra ep clef in his chin and a dimple in each cheek. He was very ıff a real mans man. He was medium height about 5' 9" and he as sharp looking, he was a sight to behold. His uniform was ıpeccable; his tailor made uniform shirt fit his muscular chest a "T." His pants were creased to perfection and his shoes were ghly shined.

Cheri had also caught his eye. Since she was standing at the ıist high counter passing out forms and talking loud he couldn't lp but notice her. After she had her people settled down and riting their information on the forms she had handed out, she ok the liberty to walk over to the area of the room where this autiful person had his prisoners standing at attention waiting eir turn to go into the court marshal room. He was pacing ck and forth slapping his baton into the palm of his hand when heri beckoned to him with her finger for him to come over to here she was standing. He came over and this was a foolish ove by him, because he was not supposed to leave his prisoners r a second. As he sauntered over to where she was standing; she oked directly at him and asked him what his name was? He id his name was Vance, she then asked him where he was from? e said he was from D.C. and he told her that he had joined the arines a year and a half ago. She said "OH" then waving him odbye she turned on her heels and walked away. As she walked ay from him she thought to herself that he has nice teeth and eat skin for a man that shaved, but he was way too cocky for her ste.

Cheri had joined the women's volley ball team for somethir
else to do besides going to that damn Club dancing like a fo
every night. This particular night they were practicing against eac
other tearing up the volley ball court, they were practicing ha
because the senior wave over physical activity felt they had a
excellent chance of winning the championship this year and wi
the way Cheri and a few others were playing, she was impresse
with what she was seeing. They were good! Cheri was knockir
the ball back and forth over the net from the back of the cou
since she was the tallest girl playing they were using her as the s
up person. Out of the corner of her eye Cheri noticed some gu
stand around against the wall watching them while they playe
and wouldn't you know it there was that guy Vance mingled wi
the bunch of them.

After the practice game was over the girls started walking ar
talking as a group as they made their way back to the wave barrack
some of the guys joined them as they walked. They were makir
introductions all around, when Vance made the comment that h
had met her earlier that day, and the rest of them better be carefu
because her conversation would drive them crazy. She looked
him and questioned him as to why he made that statement abo
her when he didn't even know her. Once they reached the wa
barracks they stood outside exchanging light banter and laughir
when out of the blue he asked her to go on a date with him. Sh
threw back her head laughing and refused and then she aske
him why do you want to go on a date with someone who driv
you crazy? Vance smirked and laughed himself, then he reache
out and took her hand and said your hands are so soft and sma
almost doll like.

She gently pulled her hand away from his and said I have part-
ne job at the base theatre and I don't have much free time. She
en told him she had to go take a shower and get ready for bed
 she said goodbye and entered the barracks. The next evening as
e was working the cash register at the base theatre she spotted
nce with his marine buddies. They exchanged greeting and he
ked her what time she got off, she said 10:30pm but once they
osed the door and started the movie and the people settled down
e would be free until closing. He asked her to join him to watch
e movie; he said he would be waiting in the balcony. So after
e closed down the concession stand for the night she went and
ined him in the balcony and they watched the rest of the movie
gether laughing out loud and eating the hot buttered popcorn
e had made fresh especially for them because the popcorn they
ld to the customers was lukewarm at best because they had to
p it early.

Before the movie ended Cheri would get up and go back down
 the concession stand, where she would count the daily receipts
d clean out the soda dispensers and wipe down the popcorn
achine; while Vance waited on the stairs outside the theatre to
alk her over to the night deposit. Then he would accompany her
 the wave barracks, where they would stand outside and talk
 they would walk over to the base bus stop and sit in the little
elter and talk, this turned into a routine for them. Vance was
nstantly asking her to be his girl and he was always trying to
ss her. But Cheri was not interested in being anybody's steady
rl because she didn't want to be pressured for sex. Besides she
dn't look at him that way, she considered him to be a friend.
meone whose company she enjoyed she felt they should keep
e relationship casual.

She didn't want to have to deal with all that heavy petting stu Sometimes when they were sitting up in the balcony watchir the movies and eating popcorn Vance would do something sl didn't understand, he would take her hand and stick her fingers his mouth and lick the salt off of them; she didn't like it becau she felt repulsed by the idea of him spitting on her hand that kir of stuff turned her off. Cheri had a clean reputation on the bas nobody could say anything bad about her morals, yes she curse like a sailor but she was not promiscuous, nobody could say the had had her sexually. She had only dated Noah exclusively ar he was seventy-five miles away and she only got to see him whe he could get off base. Which wasn't often because he was alwa standing some one else's watch and now he was out to sea f months.

Cheri was puzzled by Vance's attitude, he was always sayir negative things to her sometimes he would get mad for no reasc and call her the "Tricker", saying she was tricky that she liked play games. She wondered why he kept coming around her ar was always asking her to be his girl. She guessed it was becau she was not interested. Men always want what they can't ha and Vance was no exception. He was a year or two younger tha Cheri, so she would use that excuse all the time for not being h girl, telling him she was too old for him, that he should find a gi his own age. It would enrage him when she said it and she wou say it on purpose, just to see his reaction; and he would tighte his cute mouth into a thin line and glare at her with his da eyes before he would start walking around in circles twitching h fingers and biting his lower lip and then he would stop and s you must be crazy what is a year or two got to do with anything

Even though Cheri enjoyed his antics she sensed an underlying
ge brewing in him that she didn't like, it was something she
uldn't quite put her finger on but it was enough to make her a
tle leery of him because something was there lurking just under
e surface waiting to erupt. If she had had more experience
aling with men one on one she would have been able to realize
at Vance needed watching, he could go from hot to cold in less
an sixty seconds and he had a temper which didn't really faze
r because she had one too. She attributed his odd behavior to
n just being frustrated because he couldn't get her to say yes
his demands like he wanted her to. Cheri prided herself on
ing aloof and non-caring toward guys she didn't intend to be
mebody's fool. After spending almost every evening with Vance
a few months she got tired of him asking "no begging" her to
on a date with him to dinner and a movie.

Cheri agreed to go out with him on her next day off. Her day
came up the following week on a Tuesday; it was raining lightly
they made plans for him to pick her up from the wave barracks
6 pm. Vance arrived on time wearing civilian clothes he looked
l nice and it was the first time she had seen him out of uniform,
always wore his uniform on base and he was driving a car.
ieri asked him where he got the car; he said he had borrowed
from one of his fellow marine buddies. He had told him how
ecial this date was to him and since it was drizzling a light
n, the guy let him borrow his car so his special date wouldn't
t wet waiting around for the base bus to go into town, Cheri
s a little impressed that he felt she was so special. They went
a quaint restaurant and shared a light meal while exchanging
easant conversation, after they left the restaurant they walked
ound downtown San Francisco for a while then they stopped at
iigh end candy store and he ushered her in and purchased her
ox of candy.

Vance was the perfect gentleman, opening doors for her ar holding her arm when they crossed the street. They went into tl theatre and had to sit in the balcony since the theatre was quite fu that evening. The movie was four and a half hours long; so long had intermission. After an hour Cheri was getting bored becau it was a sword fighting epic dessert movie with men fighting ea other with swords on horseback and camels. She didn't kno what to do she was bored and kept squirming in her seat, sl wanted to ask him to leave but he had spent his money for tl tickets so she said nothing, she just sat and watched this swo fighting movie. During the movie Cheri was thinking to herse that she should have stayed on base, she should have postpon this date, tonight was not a good night, besides she was getti the cramps and her stomach and back were hurting and she w getting her monthly migraine headache.

After the movie was finally over Vance walked her back the parking garage and they got in the car and he drove the back to the base. When he drove through the gates of the ba he bypassed the way to the barracks; he didn't go to the wa barracks he started driving around looking for someplace to pa Cheri glanced over at him and told him she couldn't stay out la tonight, she had to get up early the next morning for inspectio Vance never answered her, he just nodded staring straight ahead he drove the car around, he had a plan formulated in his head; wanted to make out for real tonight, he finally had the girl of h dreams and a car, tonight he refused to take no for an answer, was tired of playing games with this girl. Cheri wasn't interest in all this driving around her stomach was cramping like crazy a she was getting irritable because she was feeling awfully moist her panties, her suspicions told her she had started her period.

Vance finally pulled the car over onto a darken road down by
e docks where the ships came in and turned off the engine. He
tinguished the headlights and turned to her with a smile and
.t his arm around her shoulders as he leaned in for a kiss. Cheri
cided she would let him kiss her a few times thinking that
ight enable her to get rid of him all she wanted to do was get to
e barracks. After she shared a few kisses with him she said she
eded to go back to the barracks now! Not in a few minutes but
ght now! Her tone had changed she was getting angry. All of a
dden Vance shoved his left hand up her skirt and when he felt
e hot moisture in her crotch area he got even more amorous.
e started trying to French kiss her breathing heavy. Cheri could
t make that fool believe that she was not horny and moist for
m! Little did he know that she had started her period and
eded to get to the barracks to put on a pad before she ruined
r clothes! The more she insisted she didn't want his advances
ile pushing his hands away the angrier he got. Vance went
llistic on Cheri, they fought like a cat and dog in the front seat
that borrowed car he felt she was just being coy, playing with
s emotions, playing hard to get but she was really not interested
him that way.

Vance grabbed her arms trying to pin her down breathing like
nadman biting on his bottom lip. When he released one of her
ms she started striking at him with all her might, hitting him
veral times in the face with her fist all the while cursing at him
d telling him to leave her alone; it must have made him madder
an a wet hen, because all of a sudden he grabbed her around
e throat with both of his hands and twisted her down into the
ivers seat of the car by her neck and started to choke and shake
r until her eyes felt so tight in her head they felt like they were
ing to pop out of their sockets.

All the while he was choking her he was saying I should ju
kill you, I should just kill you. She was on the verge of passi
out she couldn't breathe, so she went limp in his hands she h
no strength left and her breathing was shallow when he fina
released her throat. Since she was sprawled out on the seat gaspi
for air he grabbed her right arm and twisted it high up und
her head, it felt like he was trying to break it off the pain w
unbelievable but she couldn't scream because she couldn't breat
Then he straddled her right there in the front seat of the car a
with his free hand he fumbled with her clothing pushing her sk
up around her waist she was exposed except for her garter b
and stocking, then he got spastic and just started ripping away
her panties until he got tired then he just ripped them off of h
and after freeing himself from his own pants he raped her. Aft
he had satisfied himself on her limp stiff aching body, he had t
nerve to lean down and kissed her sweetly on the mouth. H
felt he had made a conquest; now she belonged to him becau
he had taken her virginity. There was the proof; the blood on t
front seat proved it, but little did he know it was from her getti
her period.

Vance rearranged his clothing and started trying to adju
her clothing as well. He had torn her panties so they were ju
dangling around her left foot there was no way she could p
them back on. She was in such pain she couldn't do anything f
herself she couldn't use her right arm and her body hurt from ju
trying to sit up. As he drove her towards the wave barracks h
kept talking to her softly asking her if she was alright, like th
were madly in love, like this horrible act had been consensu
When they reached the wave barracks she staggered ginge
out of the car not speaking a word to him and left the car do
hanging open.

She went into the barracks to her room, she was glad it was te and the lounge was closed she didn't want anyone to see her this condition. Once inside her room Cheri stripped off her othing and put on her robe, gathering her towels and soap she eaded to the shower where she stood for almost an hour letting e hot water beat down on her to try and soothe her battered ody and soul. Cheri got up when the clock radio went off, got essed and went to her job like nothing had happened the night fore, even though she was dealing with a million demons on the side. She felt that what had happened to her was not something u should share with anybody it was shameful a disgrace.

The only thing Cheri knew for sure was that she would never eak to that person again. Cheri's arm was so sore that day she uldn't type so she spent the day talking to the men at the counter out which forms to fill out. She went through her usual speech the men but her heart wasn't in her job that day, it took all she d to stay at work and she could hardly wait until 4:00pm so she uld go back to the barracks and take a hot soak in the one and ly resident bathtub and let the hot water soothe her arm and en go to bed, she ached all over her entire body and she was eeding profusely. Upon returning to the barrack that evening heri did take that hot soak in the tub and after she got out she ent to her room put on her pajamas and got into her bed and ll fast asleep.

She was awaken hours later by the volley ball team leader ho had come into her room looking for her because she had not owed up for practice that evening and they had the big game in o days. Cheri couldn't move she was so sore, her stomach ached, r head ached and her throat was sore.

She told the team leader she was sick and couldn't make it night. The team leader tried to coax her for another ten minutes get up get dressed and come to practice telling her they needed r. Cheri refused she said she was sorry to let the team down rned over and gave the woman her back and stayed in her bed d slept through the night without having any dinner.

A week later there was an announcement over the PA syster "Cheri you have a guest in the lounge", she wondered who th could be as she went down the stairs to the lounge, she wasr expecting anyone, nor did she want to be bothered with anyboc she had been spending a lot of time alone, in her room reflectir as to what she had done wrong, had she led him on, given him tl wrong ideas about her? She didn't think so.

She was just a girl who liked to have fun but it was good clea fun she didn't try to give guys the wrong impression of herself, sl wasn't that way; all she did was work and play volleyball in h spare time of which she didn't have much of. She went into tl lounge and there sat Vance.

She glared at him and started to get loud having no regar for the others in the lounge when she shouted at him what tl fuck he wanted? He jumped up from the sofa and said lets g outside and talk, grabbing her by the arm and practically draggir her to the door. They stepped out the door to stand on the porc of the barracks and folding her arms across her chest she start to rant and rave at him about what a sick bastard he was and sl didn't want to see him or have anything to do with him ever aga in life. Vance reached out trying to take Cheri's arm trying to pu her up closer to him saying how sorry he was, but she yanked away from him.

She didn't care about the tears in his eyes as she told him what nonster she thought he was. He said that he would do whatever e asked him to do to make it up to her. Then he said he didn't ıow why she was so mad, she had wanted him just as much as : had wanted her, he had felt her wet panties. Cheri recoiled :e she had been punched at his words, then she saw red as she ıpped him as hard as she could across the face before turning :r back to him and saying "kiss my ass you crazy motherfucker" 'er her shoulder as she started to walk back into the barracks ınce grabbed her around the waist to hold her still because he ınted to tell her how he really felt about her tonight. Vance said at he cared so much for her that he got caught up in the heat of ssion and completely lost his mind. Vance said he wanted to be th her for the rest of his life, that he had been to heaven with r and he wanted it to last forever, that he was crazy about her d it was all her fault because she made him nuts. She couldn't ve cared less about his apology or his bullshit, she was Noah's rl. She had only gone out with him out of boredom anyway and e was older than he was.

Vance kept pursuing her and she kept ignoring him. Some of e girls that knew about her going on a date with him noticed w he was always following her around the base questioned r why she didn't like him? Why didn't she give him a chance? ıey thought that he was gorgeous and one of her bunch the ıve name Angela even went so far as to tell Cheri if she didn't ınt him to give him to her. Vance kept showing up in places he ıew she would be just to see her, even if she wouldn't talk to him ɔking sad eyed, finally Cheri got to the place where she said oh hell with it, I'll use the dumb bastard.

She would call him and tell him to bring her a hamburg
and fries when she didn't feel like going to the mess hall, and h
would come from the other side of the base at the marine barrac
and go over to the Club place the order wait for it and then com
over to the wave barracks to bring her some food. Whatever sh
asked him to do he would do it. Cheri would go bowling with h
friends and bowl for hours and when she was finished she woul
call Vance at his barracks and tell him to come over to the Bowlin
Alley and pay for her bowling. She was using him because he fe
guilty so whatever she dished out he ate up. She would only g
to safe places with him, places that were well lighted and alwa
with others, like the Club or the Bowling Alley. She didn't tru
him to go into town and anyway going off base with him was o
of the question. Cheri's period had come and gone and Vance w
hanging around her so much kissing her ass, people were sayin
they made a good looking couple. Cheri didn't think so, and Noa
was still out to sea.

If Cheri had been more knowledgeable of physical relationshi
and the boundaries of dating she would have reported him to th
MP's because he had committed date rape, but she just wro
it off as him being so crazy about her that he couldn't contr
himself. Now everybody on the base saw them as a couple an
it didn't feel so bad to her anymore. Beside he was good lookin
and he was treating her like a queen and spending quality tim
with her, not like Noah who never had much time to act like a re
boyfriend. When they went to the Club as a couple, they wou
take their seats at a table and he would pull her chair with her
it up as close to him as possible, letting all the other guys kno
this was his girl.

Vance liked to hold her close on the slow songs so they on
danced when it was a slow song playing and it felt good being
his arms. They started going out riding around in cars with oth
couples and he would always put his arm around her and hold h
close and she would lay her head on his shoulder and enjoy th
attention from him. Vance was always kissing her hands or h
cheek, stroking her arm or her back. Cheri didn't realize it but sh
was falling for Vance, he was slowly wearing her down.

He would come over to the barracks nightly and sit with her the lounge hugging her and stealing kisses (the lounge was public place and waves are not suppose to show affection in ıblic) from her, putting love bites on her neck, she didn't know ey showed until she would go to work the next day and the men the office would say "I know what you been doing" and she ould laugh at them because she knew she wasn't doing anything rong. Sometimes when they were out on the porch at the wave ırracks she would stand behind him with her arms around his aist and her face against his shoulder and they would talk about e different things they wanted in life, she was reveling in the nstant attention from him.

Life went on but the next month Cheri started feeling strange, ıe threw up after eating her lunch one afternoon, she was tired ıd sleepy most of the time and she started craving grapes, the een ones. When it was time for her period it didn't show. Cheri ld Vance that they needed to take a walk one Saturday afternoon they walked over to the base park. When they reached the park was empty, so she sat down on top of the picnic table while he ood between her legs rubbing her hands and face because it was ıilly.

She told him what she suspected, that she wasn't feeling right ıd she might be pregnant, he said are you sure? As his eyes lit), thinking I got her now she belongs to me, she stared at him ıd said no I am not sure, I don't know what is wrong with me ıt you know what you did so there it is. After another few weeks ıssed and Cheri wasn't feeling any better, she told her friend bba who worked in the medical department what her symptoms ere. Abba gave her some pills he took from work, they were ppose to make her period come down; they only made her mpy and nervous.

Being naïve she went to the base doctor; he examined h
and scheduled another appointment and when she went back f
her next appointment she was told she was with child. Che
couldn't believe what the doctor was saying he asked her if sl
knew who the father was and she said yes and left. Cheri fe
lower than low, she knew it was all over but the shouting, th
man had come into her life and ruined her life she hated the d
she had said anything to him. She had planned on doing twen
years in the military now she was being given a discharge with
baby growing inside her. It never occurred to Cheri to turn
Vance because she was so independent, she had always handl
her own problems and she had not told a living soul what ha
happened to her, about the rape, plus knowing she was pregna
her feelings for Vance changed immediately. It was his fault. Th
weekend Cheri turned to her married friends Mia and Bea. Sl
felt that people would think she was an undercover slut comi
up pregnant, it meant her reputation wasn't as stellar as she ma
it out to be aside from cussing she was basically a nice girl wi
pretty good morals.

What Cheri couldn't get over was the fact that she was no
sexually active person and now she was with child, and sick ar
tired all the time. Her married friends had all kinds of optio
but none of them were working. The weekend she had spent wi
Bea and her husband, they fed her all kinds of pills with whisk
and made her soak in tubs of hot water for hours trying to mal
her period come down, to no avail. Monday she was back at wo
and still pregnant, since she was so slim, she was not showi
at all, she just didn't feel right. It was for real she was going
have a baby, a baby she did not want and had done nothing
get. Cheri had to do something fast this was serious but she ha
no idea what to do, she had never been in this position befor
Nobody had come up with any working solutions and she w
being discharged next week!

Boy was she mad. She only had nine months to serve before .e would have been eligible to ship over for another four years, :t the chance to go overseas and receive a signing bonus and her ıoice of duty stations anywhere in the world. She had stopped lking to Vance, she was too distressed, but she did see him the ;t day she worked at the Receiving Station, he caught up with her ı the enclosed stairway and gave her a kiss on the lips it was the reetest kiss they had ever shared and it was taboo because they ere both in uniform. Then he told her he would see her later that ght. Cheri and Vance's last night together never happened. Cheri ıs to be discharged from the military the next day so when she me in from work and took off her clothes she went straight to :d; she slept the sleep of the dead. She did not hear all the pages .e got that evening over the PA system telling her she had a guest the lounge until the lounge was closed to outsiders.

She never received any of the phone calls that were announced r her until the phones were turned off. She never knew that ınce was running all over the base that evening like a madman king different people where she was and nobody knew they ıdn't seen her. He kept coming over to the barracks constantly at evening and having her paged to no avail. She never knew out it because nobody woke her up to tell her. Where was all :r friends? The next morning she woke up and took a shower ıd dressed in one of her expensive civilian suits from Bennioff's ıd she put her hair up in a French twist, put on her patent leather ımps with matching bag, applied her makeup to perfection, rayed on some of her good perfume, closed up her luggage ıd locked it, dumped her uniforms in the box in the Barracks hief's office picked up her suitcase and went out the front door the barracks to get in her friend Mia's car, she looked fabulous. ıey drove over to the Receiving Station so Cheri could pick up :r discharge papers in silence. Mia kept stealing glances over at heri, she knew that Cheri was doing what she didn't want to do ıving in what Cheri considered a disgrace; so she reached over ıd patted her arm and said we are here for you, you have nothing worry about and don't you even think about crying when you y goodbye to those fucking people in that office.

Cheri smiled and held her head high as she went about th business of signing her discharge papers and then she bade the all farewell with a final salute, they were all extremely nice to h telling her to keep in touch, she smiled and said she would b inside she was pissed.

The Warrant Officer stood up and gave her a hug which uncommon in the military since people in uniform don't displ affection, he then told her she would be missed and he was real going to miss watching her perform for him everyday. Cheri an Mia exited the building and drove to the base bank where Che withdrew all her money she had saved from working at the ba theatre. As they drove through the gates there was that sign th she had become so use to seeing that said the same thing.

"THROUGH THESE GATES PASSES THE WORLDS FINEST",

She felt she would not be one of them again anytime soo Mia had told her husband Buck, what was going on with Che they didn't know all the circumstances of her condition but the knew she was pregnant, they thought it was Noah's baby. Bu was angry that she had made the biggest mistake ever of going the base doctors before telling him and now had been discharge They put their heads together and decided that since he worke at the medical center and was real familiar with the interns an residents there that he should ask around for some solution the problem. He asked around and found a broke resident wh needed cash yesterday and told Buck he could help them out f two hundred dollars.

If only she had let him know earlier they could have done over the weekend and she could have returned to work on Mond and nobody would have been the wiser. The only saving grace the situation would be she wouldn't be saddled with an unwante child. While Cheri and Mia were sitting around the apartme staring blankly into space, Buck called home and told them wh the plan was and after talking to him

Cheri was all for it. She had no desire to be stuck with a baby d no husband never giving any thought to Vance or how he felt out the situation. She didn't even call him and let him know ıere she was, he just never crossed her mind. In Cheri's mind s was her problem it was like she got pregnant by osmosis, and e still hadn't told Mia and Buck who the father was, she never d anybody but Vance and he was out of the picture as far as she s concerned.

That night Mia's husband brought home a man with a kit and ottle of bourbon. Cheri didn't drink but she drank that night d in a drunken haze she climbed up on top of Mia's kitchen le and let this strange man (who was a resident at the medical nter where Buck worked) insert a speculum into her vagina and en insert a tub after which he packed her with gauze, he packed r so tight it hurt. But Cheri was not complaining she needed lp and she was taking it wherever she could get it. Cheri paid m two hundred dollars of her money. The man told her he uld call her in a couple of days to check on her. But before he t her, he leaned over her and whispered in her ear "when you t straight I want some of that, you got a pretty pussy". Cheri dn't even know what this man looked like, he came and went der the cloak of darkness, using a flashlight and a hand held ht to do his business. He said this was for his own safety, he uldn't afford to lose his right to practice medicine and he wasn't en out of medical school yet

What he had said had no meaning to Cheri, she was real hig
from the bourbon, and all she wanted to do was go to bed ar
sleep, which she did for two days. Monday morning Mia left
go to work, taking her baby to the babysitters. She told Cheri s
would call when she had her break. Cheri was asleep and alo
in the apartment when she was jarred awake by the most seve
pain she had ever experienced in her young life. The pain was
strong and hard she couldn't catch her breath she had to pant
breathe and that was only the beginning, she had to deal wi
that onslaught of pain it seemed like forever. She was burning
with fever and constant racking pain and she couldn't do anythi
about it. Cheri got up from the pull out couch and tried to wa
around; this was not helping so she went and laid back down
her stomach on the couch and started to moan with the agor
The pain was so bad that she was pressing her face into the so
and digging the foam from under the cheap wall to wall carp
on the floor to keep from screaming out loud. After four or fi
hours of this constant pain, she felt like she had to use the toil
most of the time when she had the cramps it always felt better
go sit on the toilet.

Cheri staggered into the bathroom holding on to the wa
and furniture and sat down on the commode thinking she h
to make a bowel movement, then she felt all this pressure in h
groin area and she felt the only way to get some relief was to p
the tightly packed gauze out of her vagina. When she reach
down and grabbed the gauge and pulled it out the blood rush
out, and she felt something coming out of her like she was passi
the biggest blood clot she had ever passed and it fell into the toil
as she flushed the toilet, she looked back and saw the tiny embr
encapsulated in some kind of bag as it swirled down down dov
and then out of sight.

Cheri put on a sanitary napkin and went and lay down. M
called shortly there after she was on break and she asked her ho
she was doing and what was going on? Cheri told her what h
happened and she told Cheri to rest that she would be hon
soon.

When Mia arrived home Cheri was looking pretty rough, but .e was not in any pain. After some time Cheri said she felt like .e had to use the toilet again so they both went into the bathroom .d that's when this enormous blood bubble came down and was ılf stuck out of Cheri's vagina and she was starting to panic :cause she couldn't pass it!

Mia reached over and grabbed a hand full of toilet tissue and ılled it out and let it drop into the toilet, it was so big Cheri dn't think it would go down. They exchanged looks and said nultaneously that must be the afterbirth.

Cheri took a shower and washed her hair then she went and .d down. She felt better but sadden because if she had known it ould be this easy she would never have gone to the base doctor. ıe would have taken leave for a week and her life would have en back on track, but now it was too late.

She was officially discharged from the military. She could cry nor would she cry over spilled milk. That evening the inte called and asked how she was doing, she told him what she ha experienced and what had happened and he said you must hav been further along than you thought. He said if he had know that he wouldn't have touched her with a ten foot pole. Che told the intern that she had no idea how far along she had bee except that she had gotten pregnant the night she was raped ar was pregnant while having her period, which meant that she ha carried the fetus almost three months. The intern told her that th poor baby had been virtually alive at that term of her pregnancy; was not a clot of blood as she had thought and led him to believ They together, had killed a human being. Cheri felt nasty ar full of self loathing; she also felt a deep sadness for the little bal and the fact that it didn't stand a chance because of the way it w conceived. After hanging up the phone Cheri became aware the tears streaming down her cheeks and realized she was cryi as she though about the pitiful thing, then she dropped to h knees and said a prayer begging god for forgiveness for what sl had been forced to do. After a few minutes she rose to her fe went into the bathroom and got a Kleenex blew her nose and sa to herself life goes on and she refused to look back because yc can't get ahead looking back.

To be continued.